Office 2007 for Seniors

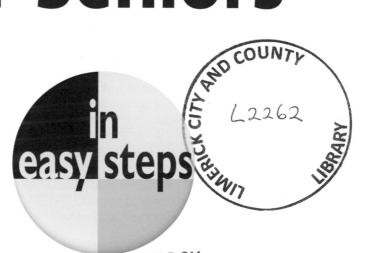

For the Over 50s

In easy steps is an imprint of In Easy Steps Limited
Southfield Road · Southam
Warwickshire CV47 0FB · United Kingdom
www.ineasysteps.com

Notice of Liability
Every effort has been made to ensure that this book
contains accurate and current information. However, In
Easy Steps Limited and the author shall not be liable for
any loss or damage suffered by readers as a result of
any information contained herein.

Trademarks
Microsoft® and Windows® are registered trademarks
of Microsoft Corporation. All other trademarks
are acknowledged as belonging to their respective
companies.

Printed and bound in the United Kingdom

ISBN 978-1-84078-379-7

Contents

Manage Data 87

Presentations 109

Manage Files 189

Up to Date and Secure 205

12 Where Next? 221

Index 235

1 Introducing Office 2007

This chapter discusses the latest version of Microsoft Office with its new style of user interface. It identifies the range of editions and outlines the requirements for installation. Also covered are the process of starting applications, the main features shared by Office applications, a summary of the new Office document types and compatibility with the older versions.

Microsoft Office 2007

Microsoft Office is a productivity suite of applications that share common features and approaches. There have been numerous versions, including Office 95, Office 97, Office 2000, Office XP (also called Office 2002) and Office 2003. The latest version, released in January 2007, is Microsoft Office 2007.

There are various editions with particular combinations of products. The Standard edition contains these applications:

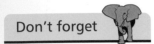

Don't forget

New PCs may come with Office 2007 Basic edition, which is like Standard but without PowerPoint. See page 222 for details of all the editions of Office.

10

- Excel 2007   Spreadsheet and data manager
- PowerPoint 2007   Presentations and slide shows
- Outlook 2007   Electronic mail and diary
- Word 2007   Text editor and word processor
- Office Tools   Diagnostics and image utilities

The Professional edition of Office contains all of these products with the addition of some business-oriented applications:

- Access 2007   Database manager
- Accounting Express 2008   USA only
- Business Contact Manager   Extension to Outlook 2007
- Publisher 2007   Professional document creation

The Ultimate edition of Office contains all of Professional, plus additional products including:

- InfoPath 2007   Database manager
- OneNote 2007   For taking notes

There's a Home and Student edition, which is like Standard, but with the OneNote application instead of Outlook. This edition is very good value, and you don't have to be a student. To illustrate the relative costs, the prices in the USA are:

Don't forget

Qualifying Microsoft products for upgrade are Works 6.0–10, Works suite 2000–2006 or later, any 2000–2007 Office program or suite and any Office XP suite except Office XP Student and Teacher.

Edition	Full	Upgrade	Licenses
Home and Student	$149	n/a	Up to three PCs
Standard	$399	$239	One or two PCs
Professional	$499	$329	
Ultimate	$679	$539	

Ribbon Technology

Whichever edition you have, the most notable feature of Office 2007 is the entirely new graphical user interface based on the Ribbon technology. This replaces the menus and toolbars that were the essence of all previous versions.

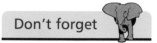

This shows the Ribbon in Word 2007, with the Home tab selected. This tab usually displays six groups associated with basic document creation - Clipboard, Font, Paragraph, Styles and Editing. Some additional contextual tabs appear when appropriate. Each group contains a set of related commands and icons.

The Ribbon contains command buttons and icons, organized in a set of tabs, each containing groups of commands associated with specific functions. The purpose is to make the relevant features more intuitive and more readily available. This allows you to concentrate on the tasks you want to perform rather than the details of how you will carry out the activities.

Some tabs appear only when certain objects are selected. These are known as contextual tabs and provide functions that are specific to the selected object, for example an inserted image:

This shows the Picture Tools Format group which is added to the Home tab in Word 2007, when you select an inserted picture.

The new user interface also features extended ScreenTips that can contain images and links to more help, as well as text. The tips are displayed when you move the mouse pointer over a command, and they describe what the commands are able to do.

What's Needed

To use Microsoft Office 2007, you will need at least the following components in your computer:

- 500 MHz processor
- 256 MB memory
- 1.5–3.0 GB available disk space
- CD-ROM or DVD drive
- 1024×768-resolution monitor
- Windows Vista or Windows XP with SP2

Some functions impose more stringent requirements, for example:

- 512 MB memory for Outlook Instant Search
- 1.0 GB memory for Word grammar and contextual spelling
- Internet connection for online help

If your computer is running Windows Vista, you'll find that the system specifications already meet or exceed requirements for Office 2007. You'll also find that the Office 2007 user interface coordinates well with the visual style of Windows Vista and Aero.

Hot tip

The larger amount of disk space is required for the more comprehensive editions of Office 2007, such as Professional or Ultimate.

Beware

These are the minimum requirements. A higher-speed processor with additional memory is the preferred configuration.

Don't forget

The illustrations in this book are usually based on Office Ultimate edition running under Windows Vista Ultimate. However, the tasks shown generally apply to any edition or operating environment.

Installing Office 2007

If you've purchased a new copy of Office 2007, you will need to install it onto your computer. Insert the supplied CD or DVD, enter the 25-character product key and accept the terms and conditions. Follow the prompts to complete the installation.

 Select Install Now to accept the default settings

Hot tip

If you have an older version of Office, you may be offered the option to upgrade the existing installation.

 Select Customize to choose how items are installed, then click a component and choose "Run all from My Computer" to include all the extras

Don't forget

Click the Microsoft Office entry and select "Run all from My Computer", to install extras for all the components.

 Select Not Available to exclude the selected component

Start an Application

When you have installed Office 2007, a new folder of shortcuts will be added to the Start Menu.

1 Select Start, All Programs

2 Select Microsoft Office to display all the installed applications

3 Select Microsoft Office Tools to display the various utilities

4 Select the application that you wish to run, for example Word 2007

14

When you start any Office application, you are reminded that you must activate your installation to fully enable all the features.

5 You can activate your copy of Office 2007 over the Internet or by telephone

The Application Window

When you start an Office application such as Excel, PowerPoint or Word, the program window is displayed with a blank document named book1, presentation1 or document1 respectively.

Office button   Quick Access toolbar   Document name   Tabs

Minimize/Restore/Close

Ribbon

Commands and icons
(display lists or galleries)

Launch button
(show dialog box)

Status bar   Scroll bars   View buttons   Zoom level

Applications such as Access and Publisher don't open a blank document but instead offer a selection of predefined application document layouts. For Publisher, these include brochures, business cards and calendars. Blank document layouts are also available.

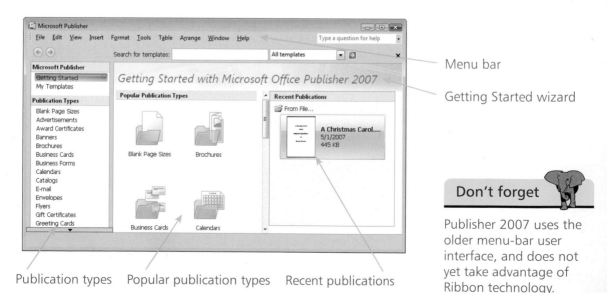

Menu bar

Getting Started wizard

Publication types   Popular publication types   Recent publications

Don't forget

Publisher 2007 uses the older menu-bar user interface, and does not yet take advantage of Ribbon technology.

Live Preview

With applications that use the Ribbon, you can see the effect on your document of formatting options such as fonts and styles, by simply pointing to the proposed change. For example, to see font formatting changes:

 1 Highlight the text that you may wish to change, and select the Home tab

2 Click the arrow next to the Font box and move the mouse pointer over the fonts you'd like to preview

3 Click the font you want, to actually apply the change to the text, or press Escape to finish viewing font options

4 You can similarly preview the alternatives provided for the Font Size, the Font Color and the Text Highlight Color options

Live Preview is available for paragraph format options (e.g. bullets, numbering and shading) and for styles.

 Highlight the text that you may wish to change, and select the Home tab

Don't forget

This facility is not available in Excel, which does not offer the Paragraph group.

2 Display the list of paragraph options, and move the mouse pointer over any that you want to preview

3 Display the list of styles (with no text selected) and preview the complete document in a variety of styles

Hot tip

The option will be previewed for the paragraph where the pointer is currently located, if no text has been selected.

17

Don't forget

You can turn off Live Preview for individual applications. Click the Office button, select the application Options, click Popular and clear the Enable Live Preview box.

Save the Document

You'll use the appropriate commands on the Ribbon for each particular application, to create and amend the application document. You should save the document periodically, to avoid the possibility of losing the work you've done.

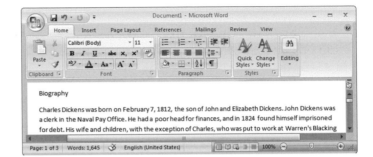

18

1 To save the document, click the Office button and select Save

2 For a document not yet named and saved, the Save As dialog opens and you can provide a name (or use the suggested name)

3 On subsequent Saves, the document will be written to disk without any further action needed

Working With the Ribbon

The Ribbon takes up a significant amount of the window space, especially when you have a lower-resolution display. To hide it:

 1 Right-click the tab row and select Minimize the Ribbon

> Customize Quick Access Toolbar...
> Show Quick Access Toolbar Below the Ribbon
> Minimize the Ribbon

2 The Office button, Quick Access toolbar and tab row will still be displayed while the Ribbon is minimized

3 The Ribbon reappears temporarily when you click one of the tabs, so you can select the required command

4 Alternatively, press and release the Alt key to display keyboard shortcuts for the tabs

5 Press Alt + shortcut key, for example Alt+P to select Page Layout, and display the Ribbon and shortcuts for that tab

Hot tip

When the application window is reduced below a certain width or depth, the Ribbon may get automatically hidden, along with the Office button, the tabs row and the Quick Access bar.

Hot tip

Repeat step 1 to redisplay the Ribbon.

Don't forget

Hold down the Alt key and press the keys in sequence, for a two-letter shortcut such as PW (Watermark). Press Esc to go back up a level.

Quick Access Toolbar

The Quick Access toolbar contains a set of commands that are independent of the selected tab. There are initially four buttons:

Save   Undo   Redo   Customize

1. Click the Save button to write the current contents of the application document to the disk drive

2. Click Undo to reverse the last action, click Redo to re-apply, and click the arrow to select several actions

   Bold
   Grow Font One Point
   Grow Font One Point
   Apply Quick Style
   Undo 2 Actions

3. Click the Customize button to add or remove icons using the list of popular commands

4. Click More Commands to display the full list of commands, then add and remove entries as desired

   Customize Quick Access Toolbar
   New
   Open
   ✓ Save
   E-mail
   Quick Print
   Print Preview
   Spelling & Grammar
   ✓ Undo
   ✓ Redo
   Draw Table
   More Commands...
   Show Below the Ribbon
   ✓ Minimize the Ribbon

20

Word Options

Popular
Display
Proofing
Save
Advanced
Customize
Add-Ins
Trust Center
Resources

Customize the Quick Access Toolbar and keyboard shortcuts.

Choose commands from:
Popular Commands

<Separator>
Accept and Move to Next
Borders and Shading...
Draw Table
Edit Footer
Edit Header
E-mail
Font...
Insert Hyperlink
Insert Page and Section Breaks
Insert Picture from File
New
New Comment
Open
Page Setup
Paragraph
Paste Special...

Customize Quick Access Toolbar:
For all documents (default)

Save
Undo
Redo

Add >>
Remove

Reset   Modify...

Show Quick Access Toolbar below the Ribbon

Keyboard shortcuts: Customize...

OK   Cancel

Office Document Types

The objects you create using the Office applications will be office documents of various types, including:

- Formatted text and graphics   Word document
- Flyers and brochures   Publisher publication
- Spreadsheets and data lists   Excel worksheet
- Presentations and slide shows   PowerPoint presentation

Each item will be a separate file. By default, these will be saved in the Documents folder for your username (logon ID).

1 To show the entries currently stored in your folder, click Start and select Documents from the list

2 Click Views, and choose Details to show the file information, including the date modified, the size and the file type

Hot tip

The files will be stored in My Documents for Office applications running under Windows XP (see page 191).

Don't forget

You can specify a different folder or create a new folder for particular documents.

Note that in some applications, groups of related items will be stored together in a specially structured file. For example:

- Data tables, queries and reports   Access database
- Messages, contacts and tasks   Outlook folders
- Notes and reminders   OneNote folders

File Extensions

To see the file extensions associated with these document types:

1 Select Start, Control Panel, click Appearance and Personalization and then click Folder Options

Appearance and Personalization
Change desktop background
Change the color scheme
Adjust screen resolution

Folder Options
Specify single- or double-click to open
Use Classic Windows folders
Show hidden files and folders

2 Click the View tab

3 Search through the list of "Advanced settings" and clear "Hide extensions for known file types"

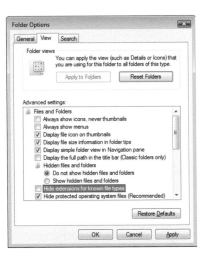

4 Click OK to apply the change to all folders

5 The file type will be shown along with the file name, whichever folder view you choose

Compatibility Mode

Office 2007 will open documents created in previous versions of Office applications, for example .doc (Word), .xls (Excel) and .ppt (PowerPoint).

1 Click the Office button and select Open, then click the down arrow for document type to list the types supported

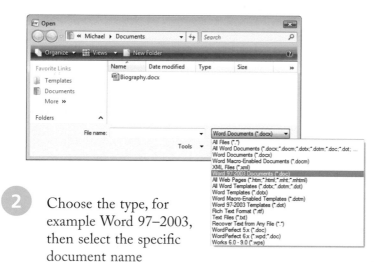

2 Choose the type, for example Word 97–2003, then select the specific document name

3 The document will be opened in Compatibility Mode

Hot tip

You may need to save documents in Compatibility Mode, as those you wish to share files with may not have Office 2007.

Don't forget

Compatibility Mode prevents the use of new or enhanced features, so the document can be used by systems with the older applications.

Convert to Office 2007

If you have opened a document in Compatibility Mode, you can convert it to Office 2007.

1 Click the Office button and select Convert

2 Click OK to confirm you want to update the document, and the compatibility restriction will be removed

3 Now, to replace the original file, click the Office button and Save, or click Save on the Quick Access toolbar

4 To retain the original document and create a new document in Office 2007 format, click the Office button and select Save As

Solving Problems

If you suffer abnormal terminations with any Office applications, Office Diagnostics will help identify and resolve the problem.

 1 Select Start, All Programs, Microsoft Office, Microsoft Office Tools and then click Microsoft Office Diagnostics

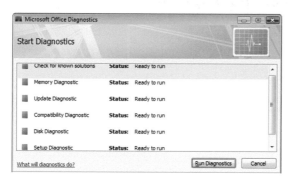

2 Click the Run Diagnostics button to start the process

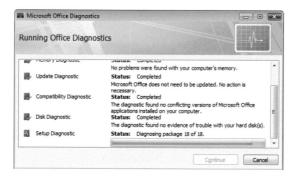

3 The diagnostics run automatically and report the findings

Hot tip

You can also start the diagnostics from the Office application. Click the Office button and select Options, Resources and Diagnose.

Beware

The tests take up to 15 minutes and you should avoid using the system while they are running.

Hot tip

The information that is displayed will depend on the findings of your diagnostic check. In this example there are no current problems, so all the tests complete successfully.

…cont'd

4 After completing Office Diagnostics, click Continue to go to Office Online for further information

5 This may tell you Update Diagnostics were unable to run

6 To enable the Update Diagnostic, click the Office button, select Options, click Trust Center, Trust Center Settings and Privacy Options and choose to download the file that helps assess problems

2 Create Word Documents

This covers the basics of word processing using the Word application in Office 2007. It covers entering, selecting and copying text, saving and autosaving, and proofing the text. It looks at the use of styles to structure the document, and at adding document features such as pictures, columns and word counts. It also discusses ways of creating tables, the use of Paste Special and the facilities for printing.

Start a Word Document

1 Right-click an empty space in a folder (e.g. Documents) and select New, Microsoft Office Word Document

Hot tip

The document will be named New Microsoft Office Word Document (though you can over-type this with a more relevant name). Double-click the file icon to open the document in Word.

2 A blank document, temporarily named Document1, will be started when you open Word (see page 14)

Don't forget

Word keeps count of all documents created during the session, and allocates the next available number.

3 If Word is already open, click the Office button, select Open, choose the blank document and click to create a document, named, for example, Document2

Enter Text

1 Click on the page, and type the text that you want. If the text is longer than a single line, Word automatically starts the new line for you

Hot tip

You can copy and paste text from other sources such as web pages. Use Paste Special (see page 45) to avoid copying styles and formats along with the text.

2 Press Enter when you need to start a new line or paragraph

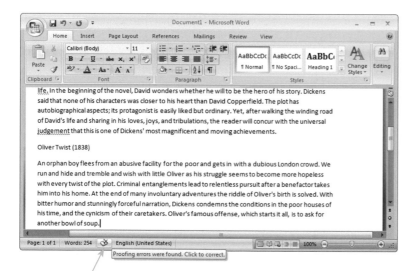

Don't forget

You may see blue underscores to indicate contextual spelling errors (misused words).

3 Proofing errors may be detected as indicated by the wavy underscores – red (spelling) or green (grammar). Click the button on the status bar to correct them one by one, or correct them all at the same time, when you've typed in the whole document (see page 33)

Select and Copy Text

It's necessary to select text for many purposes in Word, so it's not surprising that there are numerous ways to select just the amount of text you require, using the mouse or the keyboard as preferred. To select the entire document use one of these options:

1 Select the Home tab, click Select in the Editing group and then click the Select All command

2 Move the mouse pointer to the left of any text until it turns into a right–pointing arrow, then triple-click

3 Press the shortcut keys Ctrl+A

There are many mouse and keyboard options for selecting a piece of text in the body of the document. For example:

1 Double-click anywhere in a word to select the word

2 Hold down Ctrl and click anywhere in a sentence to select the whole sentence

3 To select a portion of text, click at the start, hold down the left mouse button and drag the pointer over the text

Hot tip

A single click selects just the line of text to the right of the arrow, and a double click selects the whole paragraph

Don't forget

Using the keyboard, you can press F8 to turn on Selection Mode, then press F8 once again to select the word nearest the insertion point, twice to select the sentence, three times for the paragraph and four times for the document.

You can use text selection in combination with the Clipboard tools to copy or move parts of the text. For example:

 Select a section of text using the mouse

31

2 Hold down the Ctrl key and select additional pieces of text, then select Home and click Cut in the Clipboard group

3 Click the position where the text is required and then select Home and click the Paste button

4 If you've copied several pieces of text, you may need to delete the end-of-line characters to join them up

Save the Document

When you are building a document, Word will periodically save a copy of the document, just in case a problem should arise. This minimizes the amount of text you may need to re-enter. This feature is known as AutoRecover. To check the settings:

 Click the Office button, select Word Options and click the Save option

By default, Word will save AutoRecover information every ten minutes, but you can change the frequency.

To make an immediate save of your document:

 Click the Save button on the Quick Access toolbar

 The first time, you'll be prompted to confirm the location, the file name and the document type that you want to use

 On subsequent occasions, the copy of the document on hard disk will be updated immediately, without any interaction required

Correct Proofing Errors

When you've entered all the text, you can correct proofing errors.

1 Press Ctrl+Home to go to the start of the document, then select the Review tab and click Spelling & Grammar

2 For spelling errors, choose the correct word and click Change

33

3 For terms or proper names, select Ignore All or (if the name is used often) Add to Dictionary

4 Grammar and style errors are less definitive, so you must decide about each suggestion on its merits

Change Proofing Settings

Don't forget

You can make changes to the settings for the spelling checks and for the grammar and style checks.

Hot tip

If you'd rather not use the grammar checker, clear the boxes for "Mark grammar errors as you type" and "Check grammar with spelling". Alternatively, you can hide errors in the particular document.

1 Click the Office button, select Word Options and then select the Proofing option

2 Some settings, such as "Ignore words in uppercase" and "Flag repeated words", apply to all the Office applications

3 Some settings, such as "Check spelling as you type" and "Mark grammar errors as you type", are specific to the particular Office application

Suggestions are:

seen
see
Where

4 The new contextual spelling checker in Word identifies words that are spelled correctly but used in the wrong context, and suggests alternative words that might be more appropriate

Apply Styles

1 Click the main heading and select Style Heading 1

Don't forget

You can change the style for parts of the text to suit the particular contents, using the Styles group on the Home tab.

2 Click one of the subsidiary headings and select Heading 2

Hot tip

Click the down arrow to show the next row of styles

3 Click in the text paragraph and select No Spacing

Don't forget

Apply these two styles to other headings and paragraphs. To repeat a style, select an example, double-click the Format Painter icon and then click each similar item in turn.

Outline View

When you have structured the document using headings, you can view it as an outline:

1 Select the View tab and click the Outline button to switch to Outline view and enable the Outlining tab

2 In the Outline Tools group click the box labelled Show First Line Only, so that you can see more entries at once

This makes it easier for you to identify any entries that are out of order. In this example the entries for David Copperfield and Oliver Twist are out of chronological sequence.

…cont'd

Outline view also makes it easy for you to reposition selected entries.

 1 Click the arrow next to Show Level, and choose Level 2

2 Click an entry, e.g. David Copperfield, and click the down arrow to move it

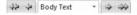

3 The selected entry, with all its subsidiary levels and text, will move one row for each click of the arrow button

Insert a Picture

1 Position the typing cursor at the location where the item is required, inserting a blank line if desired

2 Select the Insert tab and click the appropriate icon or command, for example Picture (in the Illustrations group)

3 Locate the file for the picture, and click the Insert button

You can adjust the position of the picture on the page of text.

1 Click the Position button in the Arrangements group and move the pointer over the buttons

2 A live preview will be displayed. Click the appropriate button for the position you prefer

3 Click the up or down arrow on the height to adjust the size of the picture. The width is changed proportionally

Page Layout

The Page Layout tab allows you to control how the document contents are placed on the page, by just clicking one of the function commands in the Page Setup group.

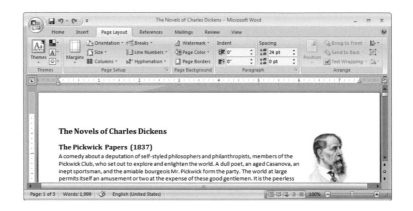

1 Click the Orientation command to select Portrait or Landscape

2 Click the Size command to select the paper size from the list, or click More Paper Sizes to show other choices, including the Custom Size option

3 Click the Margins command to choose one of the predefined setups, or click Custom Margins to display the Page Setup dialog and enter specific values

Display in Columns

1 Select the text you wish to put into columns, click the Page Layout tab and select Columns from Page Setup

41

2 Choose the number of columns required

3 Click anywhere in the body text, select the Home tab, click Select, Select Text with Similar Formatting and then click the Justify button

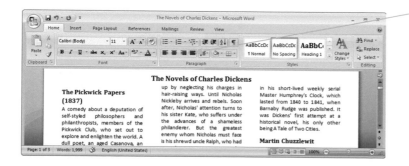

Word Count

If you are preparing a document for a publication, such as a club magazine, you may need to keep track of the number of words you've produced. Word 2007 makes this easy to do.

1 At any time, you can view the latest word count on the status bar

2 Click the word count to display further details of the content

For more information, turn on Readability Statistics, which assess the complexity of the contents.

3 Select the Review tab and click Spelling & Grammar in the Proofing group

4 After the spelling check, the statistics are displayed

Create a Table

To specify a table in your document:

 1 Click the point where you want the table, then click the Insert tab and select Table

2 Move the pointer over the Insert Table area to select the number of rows and columns, then click to confirm

Book Title	Published	Lines of Text	Total Words	Variety of Words
The Pickwick Papers	1837	30203		

 3 Enter the required contents. Press the Tab key to move to the next cell in the table

Book Title	Published	Lines of Text	Total Words	Variety of Words
The Pickwick Papers	1837	30203	309327	14850
Oliver Twist	1838	14998	162760	10321
Nicholas Nickleby	1839	29642	328994	14579
The Old Curiosity Shop	1841	18284	221854	12024

Hot tip

You'll see previews of the indicated table sizes, as you move the pointer across the Insert Table area.

Don't forget

Press the arrow keys to navigate around the table. Click and drag a separator line to adjust the width of a column.

Convert Text

If you already have the text that's needed for the table, taken from another document perhaps, you can convert the text into a table.

1 Make sure that the cell entries are separated by a tab mark or some other unique character

2 Highlight the text, select the Insert tab and then click Table, Convert Text to Table

3 Specify your particular separation character and then click OK

4 The table will be created with the data inserted into the relevant cells

Book Title	Published	Lines of Text	Total Words	Variety of Words
The Pickwick Papers	1837	30203	309327	14850
Oliver Twist	1838	14998	162760	10321
Nicholas Nickleby	1839	29642	328994	14579
The Old Curiosity Shop	1841	18284	221854	12024
Barnaby Rudge	1841	21338	259882	12834
Martin Chuzzlewit	1844	29880	345528	15350
Dombey and Son	1848	30933	357890	15032
David Copperfield	1850	30264	363472	13890
Bleak House	1853	30684	362012	15057
Hard Times	1854	9173	105607	8741
Little Dorrit	1857	28973	344932	14786
A Tale of Two Cities	1859	12810	138150	9732
Great Expectations	1861	15906	189173	10733
Our Mutual Friend	1865	33143	333784	14979
The Mystery of Edwin Drood	1870	11840	95944	9103

Paste Special

To copy the text without including its formatting and graphics:

 1 Highlight the text you want, then right-click the selected area and click the Copy command

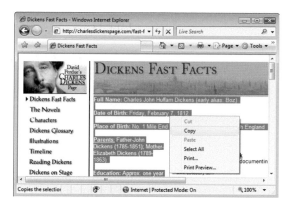

2 Click in the document where the text is to appear, select the Home tab, and click the arrow below the Paste button

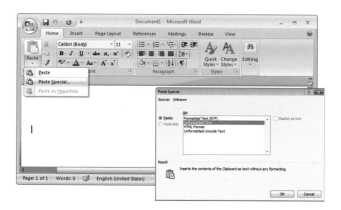

3 Click Paste Special and choose Paste, Unformatted Text

Hot tip

When you copy information from other documents or from web pages, the text may include graphics, formatting and colors that are inappropriate for your document.

Beware

Graphical information won't be copied, even if it has the appearance of text (as with the "Dickens Fast Facts" title of the text being copied for this example).

Don't forget

The copied text will inherit the format of that part of the document where you clicked before carrying out the paste operation.

Print Document

To print a document from within Word:

1 Click the Office button and select Print (or press Ctrl+P)

2 Select the printer to use, adjust options such as the specific pages to be printed print and the number of copies required, then click OK to begin the printing

3 To print a single copy of the whole document on the default printer, click Office, click the arrow next to Print and then select Quick Print

3 Complex Documents

Microsoft Word can be used to create and edit more complex documents such as booklets and brochures. This chapter covers importing text, inserting illustrations, creating tables of contents and illustrations. It shows how templates can be used to help create documents. It also introduces Publisher, the Office application that is specifically designed for desktop publishing.

Start a Booklet

To illustrate some of the facilities available for creating and organizing complex documents, we'll go through the process of importing and structuring the text for a booklet. In this example we use *A Christmas Carol* by Charles Dickens.

Hot tip

The text for books that are in the public domain can be found on the Internet at websites such as Project Gutenberg at www.gutenberg.org.

1 Start by typing the book title, author and chapter names

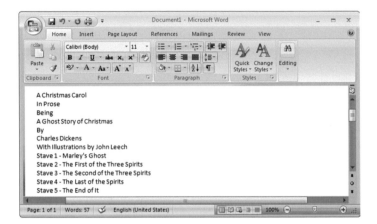

2 Set the language. This is a UK English book, so press Ctrl+A to select the text, click the Language button on the status bar and pick English (United Kingdom)

Beware

You need to highlight all the text, to change to a different language for the whole document.

Don't forget

By default, the first line of text will be used as the name for the document, in this case "A Christmas Carol".

3 Click Save on the Quick Access toolbar, and provide a name for the document, or accept the suggested name

Choose Page Arrangement

Before adding more text, set the paper size and the margins.

 Select the Page Layout tab, and click Size to choose paper size, e.g. Letter

 Click Margins and choose the Custom Margins option

 From the Page Setup dialog, in the Pages section, select "Multiple pages", "Book fold"

Specify the number of sheets per booklet (in multiples of 4 up to 40) or choose All to assemble the document as a single booklet

Hot tip

For a book or brochure, you may want to arrange the pages in the form of booklets.

Don't forget

The orientation changes to landscape, and you get four pages of the document on each piece of paper (printed on both sides). A four-sheet booklet, for example, would be printed as:

Front

Back

Create the Structure

1 Highlight the text for the chapter titles

2 Click the Home tab and select Quick Styles, Heading 1

(see page 52)

3 With the chapter titles still selected, click the Center button in the Paragraph group

4 To replace hyphens by line breaks in the chapter titles, click the Editing button and select Replace, again with the chapter tiles selected

5 In the "Find what" box, type a hyphen with a space either side, that is " - " (without the quotation marks)

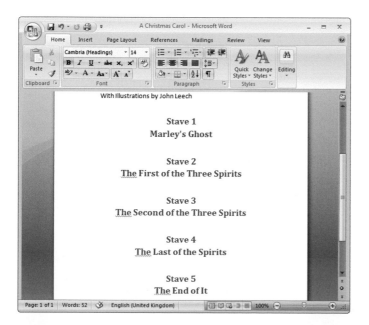

6 In the "Replace with" box, type "^l" (this is the control code for a manual line break)

7 This changes all the occurrences in the selected text. Click No to skip the remainder of the document, to avoid changing hyphens elsewhere in the text

Hot tip

You can click the More button and select Special, Manual Line Break to insert the required code.

Don't forget

To see the line-break codes, click the Show/Hide button (in the Paragraph group on the Home tab). Note that each title remains a single item, even though spread over two lines.

**Stave·1↵
Marley's·Ghost¶**

Import Text

1 Click just to the right of the Stave 1 title and select Insert, Page Break to start the chapter on a new page

2 Click the page, just past the end of the title, and press Enter, to add a new blank line (in Body Text style)

3 Select Insert, click Insert Object and choose Text from File

4 Locate the file holding the required text and click Insert

5 Click OK to select the appropriate encoding, if prompted

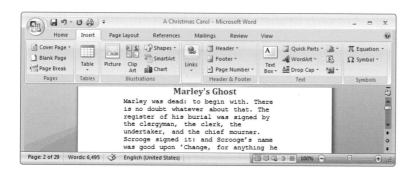

The text will be copied to the document at the required location.

6 Click anywhere in the new text, click the Home tab, then click Select, and choose Select Text with Similar Formatting

7 Select your preferred style, e.g. Normal, No Spacing

8 All the text inserted into the document will be converted to the selected style

Insert Illustrations

1 Find the location for an illustration: for example, select Home, click Find and search for the appropriate text, such as "Figure: "

Hot tip

The text contains the titles for the illustration at the required locations, in the form: "Figure: Title of Illustration".

2 For each location, select the Insert tab and click Picture

Don't forget

You can insert pictures from image files of all the usual types, including bitmap, jpeg (photos) and gif (web graphics).

3 Locate the file containing the required illustration and click Insert

4 The picture is inserted into the document, in line with the text, and you can adjust its position

Add Captions

Don't forget

Repeat these steps to insert a picture and a caption for each of the illustrations in the book.

Don't forget

If the document doesn't already contain the title for the illustration, type it after the automatic number in the Caption box or directly into the document.

55

1. From the Reference tab, select Insert Caption and click OK

2. After the automatic number, type a colon ":" and insert the text for the picture title

Hot tip

The captions that you add are used to create a table of illustrations (see page 58).

Table of Contents

When you have formatted text within the document with heading levels you can use these to create and maintain a contents list.

1 Click the Page Number button on the Status bar, type "2" and click Go To, then Close, to move to that page

Don't forget

You could also select Insert, Page Break, to provide a new blank page ahead of the typing-cursor location.

2 Select the Insert tab and click Blank Page in the Pages group, to insert a blank page for the contents list

Beware

Move to the new page (press the back arrow, or use the Go To command) to go to the new page 2, before selecting the Table of Contents button.

3 On the References tab, click the Table of Contents button

④ Choose the type of table that you want, for example Automatic Table 1 (with "Contents" as the title)

Hot tip

This type of table will use heading levels 1, 2 and 3 to generate the table. You can also build a table using custom styles, or based on manually selected text.

⑤ The table of contents is inserted. When it is selected, you can see that it is built up from field codes

Beware

The table of contents must be updated to show any changes to the heading-text content or the page-number value.

Don't forget

When you hover the mouse pointer over an entry in the table, with the shift key pressed, you'll have a link to the associated section of the document.

Table of Illustrations

1 Go to the start of chapter 1 and insert another blank page, this time for a list of illustrations

Entries for the chosen caption type, in this case figures, will be identified and included in the table.

2 On the new page, type "Illustrations", select the Home tab, the arrow to expand the Styles group, and Heading 2

3 Press Enter to add a blank line, then on the References tab click Insert Table of Figures

References

Insert Table of Figures
Update Table
Insert Caption   Cross-reference
Captions

4 Clear the box "Include label and number" if desired

5 Click OK to insert the table of figures

6 The table of figures is similar to the table of contents

 7 Click the table to see field codes and links to the figures

8 Highlight the whole table and select Toggle Field Codes

Insert Preface

1 Go to page 2 (the contents page) and insert a blank page for the book preface

2 On the new page, type "Preface", select the Home tab, the arrow to expand the Styles group, and Heading 2

3 Press Enter and insert text from a file (see page 52) or type the text for the preface

4 Adjust the formatting and alignment of the text as desired, for example selecting Justify for the main portion and Increase Indent for the signature section

5 Select Save on the Quick Access toolbar

Update Table of Contents

When you make changes, such as the preface or the illustrations list, that include new headings (level 1, 2 or 3), the table of contents is affected. However, the updates will not be displayed immediately. To apply the updates:

 1 Locate the table of contents and click anywhere within it

2 Select "Update entire table" and click OK

3 The new entries will be inserted, and the page numbers will be updated as appropriate

Hot tip

Whenever you add text to the document, or insert pages, the page numbers for the entries in the table of contents change, but the changes will not appear until you explicitly select Update Table.

Don't forget

If you've added pages or text to your document, but not changed the headings, select "Update page numbers only".

61

Decorate the Page

Hot tip

Finally, you can enhance the formatting of the title page, using styles or WordArt.

1 Select sections of text and choose the appropriate format

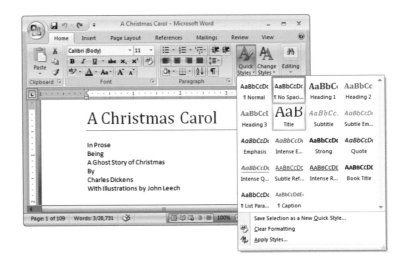

2 For example, select the book title and choose the Title style. There are also Subtitle and various Emphasis styles

Title style

Subtitle style

Intense Emphasis

3 For more impact, select the item of text and from the Insert tab choose the WordArt option in the text group

1 Pick the style of WordArt to try (you can change it later)

2 Choose the font, for example Old English, set the size and attributes and edit the text if desired

3 The text is inserted using the WordArt style selected

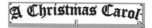

Templates

1 Click the Office button, select New, and choose "New from existing", or select an installed template

2 For a new requirement, select the relevant Office Online category (and subcategory if offered); use the thumbnail and preview images to choose the most suitable template

3 Click the Download button for the required template.
Your Office software is validated before the transfer starts

Don't forget

Each time you download from the Office Online website, your Office software is automatically checked. Click the box to hide the message for future downloads.

4 When the transfer completes, a new document is opened using the chosen template

5 Change the contents of the text boxes to personalize the document

Don't forget

A two-fold document such as this greetings card will have part of the contents inserted upside down, so that it appears correctly after printing and folding.

65

6 In future you can select New, My Templates to use the template to create another document of that type

Hot tip

When you download a template, it is added to My Templates (and to Recent Templates) so that you won't have to download it the next time it's needed.

Publisher

Don't forget

Publisher uses the menu and toolbar structure used in previous versions of Office, rather than the new Ribbon technology.

Microsoft Office Publisher 2007

Hot tip

You can prepare your text in Word, which has superior text-entry capabilities, then import the Word documents into Publisher to create the final publication.

Don't forget

Customize the template before you use it to create your document, or make the changes later, in the document itself.

1   Start the Publisher application, if included in your edition of Office, to see the range of publication types supported

Publisher provides a higher level of desktop publishing capability, with a great variety of paper sizes and styles, many templates for brochures and leaflets etc., and lots of guidance.

2   For example, select the Greeting Cards category, and click the Congratulations card type

3   Click any template in the group to see an enlarged version and details of the color and font schemes

Create a Publication

1 Choose the template you want to use, for example Congratulations 2, and click the Create button

2 Click the link "Select a suggested verse", to review examples of sample text, then click OK to choose one

3 Click section 2 or 3 to see the middle portion of the card

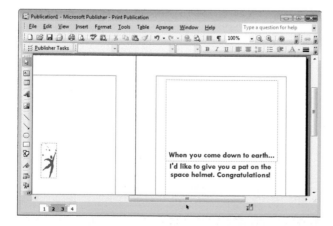

Print the Publication

1 Click section 4 to see the back portion of the card

2 Select File, Print Preview, to see how it will appear on paper

3 The document is shown as a single full page, with sections 2 and 3 inverted

4 Calculations

This looks at Excel, the spreadsheet application, and covers creating a new workbook, entering data, replicating values, formatting numbers, adding formulas and functions and using templates.

Start Excel

To start Microsoft Excel with a fresh new spreadsheet:

1 Click Start, All Programs, Microsoft Office and select Microsoft Office Excel 2007 to open with Book1

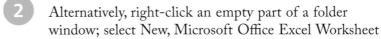

70

2 Alternatively, right-click an empty part of a folder window; select New, Microsoft Office Excel Worksheet

3 Double-click the file icon New Microsoft Office Excel Worksheet to display and edit the document

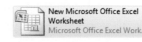
New Microsoft Office Excel Worksheet
Microsoft Office Excel Work...

The spreadsheet presented is an Excel workbook that contains, initially, three worksheets, each of which is blank. The cells that it contains are empty – all 17 million of them.

Hot tip

There can be up to 1048576 rows and 16384 columns. This compares with 65536 rows and 256 columns in previous releases.

1 To move to the last row (1048576) in the worksheet, press End and then press the down arrow

2 To move to the last column (XFD) in the worksheet, press End and then press the right arrow

If the worksheet contains data, the action taken depends on the initial location.

Beware

It may be impractical to utilize even a fraction of the total number of cells available, but the enlarged sheet size does give greater flexibility in designing spreadsheets.

3 If the selected cell contains data, pressing End and then an arrow key takes you to the edge of the data area

4 If the current cell is empty, you move to the start of the adjacent data area

Don't forget

The movement is always in the direction of the arrow key selected.

5 If there's no more data in that direction, you'll move to the edge of the worksheet, as with an empty worksheet

71

Enter Data

The most common use of spreadsheets is for financial planning, for example to keep track of income and expenditure. To create a family budget:

1 Open a blank worksheet, select cell A1 and type the title for the spreadsheet, e.g. "Family Budget"

2 Press the Enter or down key to insert the text and move to cell A2, and type the next entry, "Income"

72

3 Repeat this process to add the remaining labels for the income and expense items you want to track

If you omit an item, you can insert an additional worksheet row. For example, to include a second "Salary" income item:

1 Click a cell (e.g. C4) in the row that's just below where the new entry is required and select Insert, Insert Sheet Rows from the Cells group on the Home tab

2 Enter the additional label, e.g. "Salary 2nd", in A4

3 Double-click an existing cell to edit or retype the entry, for example to change "Salary" to "Salary 1st" in A3

Quick Fill

You can create one column of data, then let Excel replicate the cell contents for you. For example:

1 Enter monthly values in column C, for example "January" in C2 and values in cells C3–C7 and C10–C15

2 Highlight cells C2–C15, move the mouse pointer over the box at the bottom right, and when it becomes **+** then drag to the right to replicate the cells for further months

74

3 Release the mouse pointer when the required number of columns is indicated

	A	B	C	D	E	F	G	H	I
1	Family Budget								
2	Income		January	February	March	April	May	June	
3	Salary 1st		1000	1000	1000	1000	1000	1000	
4	Salary 2nd		750	750	750	750	750	750	
5	Royalties		200	200	200	200	200	200	
6	Dividends		100	100	100	100	100	100	
7	Interest		150	150	150	150	150	150	
8	Total Income								
9	Expenses								
10	Auto		200	200	200	200	200	200	
11	Clothing		150	150	150	150	150	150	
12	Entertainment		125	125	125	125	125	125	
13	Living		950	950	950	950	950	950	
14	Insurance		300	300	300	300	300	300	
15	Miscellaneous		400	400	400	400	400	400	
16	Total Expenses								
17	Net Balance								

4 Numeric values are duplicated, but the month name is detected, and the succeeding months are inserted

After you've used the Fill handle, the Auto Fill Options button appears. Click this to control the action, for example to replicate the formatting only, or to copy cells without devising a series.

- Copy Cells
- Fill Series
- Fill Formatting Only
- Fill Without Formatting
- Fill Months

5 When you've entered data into the worksheet, remember to periodically click the Save button on the Quick Access toolbar to store the file

Save As

File name: Family Budget

Save as type: Excel Workbook

Authors: Michael
Tags: Add a tag
Title: Add a title

Subject: Specify the subject
Manager: Specify the manager
Company: Specify the company name

☐ Save Thumbnail

 Browse Folders

Tools ▾ | Save | Cancel

Don't forget

Having initialized the cells, you can edit or replace the contents of any cells to complete the information needed.

Hot tip

Excel detects weekdays to create a series such as Monday, Tuesday ...; and it detects abbreviated names such as Jan, Feb ... or Mon, Tue ....

Don't forget

The first time you click the Save button, you'll be prompted to provide a file name in place of the default Book1.

Sums and Differences

When you've entered the data and made the changes required, you can introduce functions and formulas to complete the worksheet.

1 Click cell C8 (total income for January), then select the Home tab and click the Sum button

76

2 Press Enter to show the total, then repeat the procedure for cell C16 (total expenses for January)

3 Click in cell C17 (net balance for January)

4 Type "=", click C8, type "-", click C16 (to calculate total income for January minus total expenses for January)

Hot tip

The = symbol indicates that the following text is a formula. You can type the cell references, or click on the cell itself and Excel will enter the appropriate reference.

	A	B	C	D	E	F	G	H	I
7	Interest		150	150	150	150	150	150	
8	Total Income		2500						
9	Expenses								
10	Auto		200	200	200	200	200	200	
11	Clothing		150	150	150	150	150	150	
12	Entertainment		125	150	175	125	50	125	
13	Living		950	950	950	950	950	950	
14	Insurance		300	300	300	300	300	300	
15	Miscellaneous		400	400	400	400	400	400	
16	Total Expenses		2125						
17	Net Balance		=C8-C16						

(Formula bar: SUM =C8-C16)

5 Press Enter to complete the formula and display the result

6 Select cell C8 and use the Fill handle to replicate the formula for the other months (e.g. February to June), and repeat this process for cells C16 and C17

(Formula bar: C17 =C8-C16)

	A	B	C	D	E	F	G	H	I
1	Family Budget								
2	Income		January	February	March	April	May	June	
3	Salary 1st		1000	1000	1000	1000	1000	1000	
4	Salary 2nd		750	750	750	750	750	750	
5	Royalties		500	300	100	50	0	500	
6	Dividends		100	100	100	150	150	150	
7	Interest		150	150	150	150	150	150	
8	Total Income		2500	2300	2100	2100	2050	2550	
9	Expenses								
10	Auto		200	200	200	200	200	200	
11	Clothing		150	150	150	150	150	150	
12	Entertainment		125	150	175	125	50	125	
13	Living		950	950	950	950	950	950	
14	Insurance		300	300	300	300	300	300	
15	Miscellaneous		400	400	400	400	400	400	
16	Total Expenses		2125	2150	2175	2125	2050	2125	
17	Net Balance		375	150	-75	-25	0	425	

(Status bar: Average: 141.6666667 Count: 6 Sum: 850)

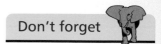

Don't forget

When the formula is replicated, the cell references, e.g. C8:C16, are incremented, to D8:D16, E8:E16 etc.

Formatting

1 Click A1 (the title cell), then select the Home tab, choose a larger font size, and select a font effect such as Bold

2 Press Shift and click H1 to highlight the row across the data, then click the Merge and Center button

	A	B	C	D	E	F	G	H
1				Family Budget				
2	**Income**		January	February	March	April	May	June
3	Salary 1st		1000	1000	1000	1000	1000	1000
4	Salary 2nd		750	750	750	750	750	750
5	Royalties		500	300	100	50	0	500
6	Dividends		100	100	100	150	150	150
7	Interest		150	150	150	150	150	150
8	**Total Income**		2500	2300	2100	2100	2050	2550
9	**Expenses**							
10	Auto		200	200	200	200	200	200
11	Clothing		150	150	150	150	150	150
12	Entertainment		125	150	175	125	50	125
13	Living		950	950	950	950	950	950
14	Insurance		300	300	300	300	300	300
15	Miscellaneous		400	400	400	400	400	400
16	**Total Expenses**		2125	2150	2175	2125	2050	2125
17	**Net Balance**		375	150	-75	-25	0	425

3 Click the Categories and Totals labels (e.g. A2, A8, A9, A16, A17) and change the font size and effects

4 Alternatively, click Styles to pick a suitable cell style

...cont'd

To emphasize the "Net Balance" values for each month:

1 Select the range of cells, e.g. C17:H17

2 Select Styles, Conditional Formatting, Color Scales and choose for example the Green–Yellow–Red color scale

3 The cells are colored according to the values

Rounding Up

You can use Excel to help you solve numerical problems, such as the number of tiles needed to cover the floor area of a room.

1 Open a new, blank worksheet and enter these labels in the first column:
Number of Tiles
Tile Length
Tile Width
Room Length
Room Width
Number
Per Box
Boxes

2 Enter sample sizes in cells B2:B5, making sure that you use the same units for the tile and the room dimensions

3 In cell B6 type the formula "=(B4/B2)*(B5/B3)"

4 In cell B8 type the formula "=B6/B7"

However, if you try to fit the tiles to the area, you'll find that some tiles have to be cut. The wastage leaves part of the area uncovered.

To ensure that there are enough whole tiles to completely cover the area, you need to round up the evaluations:

1 Copy B2:B8 to C2:C8, and in cell C6 type the formula "=CEILING(B4/B2,1)*CEILING(B5/B3,1)"

Hot tip

The CEILING function rounds the results up to the next significant value, in this case the next highest integer. If the tiles have a repeat pattern, you might need to use the pattern size as the significant number.

The number of whole tiles increases to 42, which will now cover the complete floor area, even after cutting.

This gives 5.25 boxes. Assuming that boxes must be purchased in whole numbers, this result also needs rounding up.

2 Copy C2:C8 to D2:D8, and in cell D8 type the formula "=ROUNDUP(D6/D7,0)" to get the result: 6 boxes

Don't forget

This rounds up the result to zero decimal places, which gives the next highest integer.

Find a Function

There are a large number of functions available in Excel, so they are organized into a library of groups to make it easier to find the one you need.

Hot tip

Clicking the More Functions button will display a secondary list of categories.

1 Select the Formulas tab to show the Function Library

2 Click a category in the Function Library for an alphabetic list of functions it offers

Don't forget

You can also click the Insert Function button on the formula bar.

3 If you don't know where to search for the function you want, click the Insert Function button in the Function Library

Hot tip

Enter keywords related to the activity you want to perform, and Excel will list all potentially relevant functions.

4 Choose a category and pick a function from the list

5 Alternatively, type a description and click Go, then select one of the recommended functions

Don't forget

The function arguments for the selected function are shown and a brief description is provided.

6 Select a suitable function, e.g. PMT, and click OK

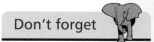
83

7 Type the values for the arguments (Rate, Nper, etc.) using the description provided as you select each item

Hot tip

You can optionally provide a final value Fv (the cash balance), and also specify the Type (payments made at the start or the end of each period).

8 The result is displayed (a negative figure, indicating a payment) and the function is inserted into the worksheet

Goal Seeking

Using the PMT function, you can establish the monthly payments required to pay off a long-term loan over, say, 25 years.

Hot tip

To calculate payments for an interest-only loan, set Fv (see page 83) to the same value as the loan amount.

B6 ▾ ƒx =PMT(B2/12,B4*B3,B5,0,0)

Loan Repayments

	A	B
2	Rate (pa)	7.50%
3	Payments (pa)	12
4	Years	25
5	Loan Amount	150000
6	Payment (pm)	($1,108.49)

Suppose, however, you'd like to know how many years it will take to pay off the loan, if you increase the payments to, say, $1500.

1 One way to establish this is by trial and error, adjusting the number of years until you get the required payment

E4 ▾ ƒx 10

Loan Repayments

	A	B	C	D	E
2	Rate (pa)	7.50%	7.50%	7.50%	7.50%
3	Payments (pa)	12	12	12	12
4	Years	25	20	15	10
5	Loan Amount	150000	150000	150000	150000
6	Payment (pm)	($1,108.49)	($1,208.39)	($1,390.52)	($1,780.53)

Don't forget

You would carry on refining your estimate, e.g. trying 12 then 14 to discover that the correct answer lies between these two periods.

2 Try 20 years, then 15 years, then 10 years, and the payment then goes above $1500. So the appropriate period would be between 10 and 15 years

However, Excel provides an automatic way to apply this type of process, and this can give you an exact answer very quickly.

1 Click the cell containing the function, select the Data tab and click the What If Analysis button in Data Tools

Hot tip

Use the Scenario Manager to create a set of results for a range of values, such as 10, 15 and 20 years of repayments.

2 Select the Goal Seek option and specify the required result –1500 (payment per month) and the changing cell B4 (number of years)

85

3 Goal Seeking tries out various values for the changing cell, until the desired solution is found

Beware

You must specify the target payment as a negative value since it is a repayment, otherwise Goal Seeking will be unable to find a solution.

4 Click OK to return to the worksheet with its revised results

Templates

Hot tip

You can get started with your worksheet by using one of the ready-made templates that are offered for many common requirements.

1 Select the Office button and click the New button

2 Select Installed Templates or "My Templates" to choose from the list of templates already on your system

3 Select a category to review the templates on Microsoft Office Online, and click Download to install

Don't forget

Your Office software will be automatically validated (see page 65) when you choose to download an item.

5 Manage Data

Excel also manages data, so we look at importing data, applying sorts and filters, and selecting specific sets of data. The data can be used to create a chart, or you can arrange the data in tables, insert totals and computations and look up values. For more advanced requirements, some editions of Office include Access, which offers full database management functions.

Import Data

You don't always need to type in all the information in your worksheets, if the data is already available in another application. For example, to import data from a delimited text file:

1 Click the Office button and select Open

2 Select the file that contains the data you wish to import and click Open to start the Text Import Wizard, which recognizes the delimited file. Click Next to continue

3 Choose the delimiter (e.g. Comma) and click Next

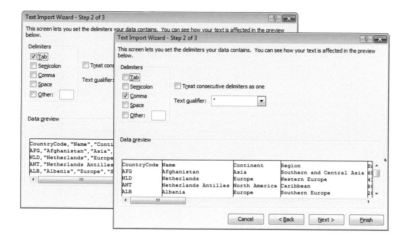

Hot tip

When you choose a delimiter, you can see the effect on the text in the preview area.

4 Adjust column formats if required, then click Finish

Don't forget

The default format is General, which will handle most situations, but you can select specific data formats where appropriate.

89

5 The data is presented in the form of an Excel worksheet

Explore the Data

1 Double-click or drag the separators between columns to reveal more of the data that they contain

	A	B	C	D	E
1	CountryCode	Name	Continent	Region	SurfaceArea
2	AFG	Afghanistan	Asia	Southern and Central Asia	652090
3	NLD	Netherlands	Europe	Western Europe	41526
4	ANT	Netherlands Antilles	North America	Caribbean	800
5	ALB	Albania	Europe	Southern Europe	28748

2 Select the View tab, click Freeze Panes in the Window group and select Freeze Top Row

	A	B	C		F
1	CountryCode	Name	Continent		ndepYea
2	AFG	Afghanistan	Asia		191
3	ALB	Albania	Europe		191
4	DZA	Algeria	Africa		196
5	ASM	American Samoa	Oceania	Polynesia	199
6	AND	Andorra	Europe	Southern Europe	468	127
7	AGO	Angola	Africa	Central Africa	1246700	197
8	AIA	Anguilla	North America	Caribbean	96
9	ATA	Antarctica	Antarctica	Antarctica	13120000

Unfreeze Panes Unlock all rows and columns to scroll through the entire worksheet.

Freeze Top Row Keep the top row visible while scrolling through the rest of the worksheet.

Freeze First Column Keep the first column visible while scrolling through the rest of the worksheet.

3 Press Ctrl+End to move to the last cell in the data area

	D	E	F	G	H	I	J	K	L	M
1	Region	SurfaceAr	Ind(	Popu	LifeEx	GNP	GovernmentForm	HeadOfState	Cap	Code2
236	Eastern Africa	78		0		0	Dependent Territory	Elisabeth II		IO
237	Antarctica	3903		0		0	Dependent Territory	Elisabeth II		GS
238	Antarctica	359		0		0	Territory of Australia	Elisabeth II		HM
239	Antarctica	7780		0		0	Nonmetropolitan Ter	Jacques Chirac		TF
240	Micronesia/Caribbean	16		0		0	Dependent Territory	George W. Bush		UM

Sort

1 Click a cell in the "Name" column, select the Data tab and click the A–Z (ascending) button to sort by name

91

Don't forget

You can also select the Sort options from within the Editing group on the Home tab.

2 Click a cell in the "Population" column and click the Z–A (sort descending) button, to sort from highest to lowest

Hot tip

Excel automatically selects all the surrounding data and sorts whole rows into the required order.

3 To sort by more than one value, click the Sort button

Don't forget

You can sort the data into sequence using several levels of values.

Beware

If a selection of the worksheet is highlighted when you click one of the buttons, the sort may be restricted to the selected data.

4 Click the arrow in the "Sort by" box and select the main sort value, for example "Continent"

5 Click the Add Level button and select the additional sort values, for example "Region" and then "Population"

Don't forget

For data organized by columns rather than rows, click the Options button and select "Sort left to right".

6 Change the sort sequence if needed, then click OK to sort the data by population within region and continent

Filters

You can filter the data to hide the entries that are not of immediate interest.

 1 Click a cell within the data area, select the Data tab and click the Filter button in the Sort & Filter group

Hot tip

You can also select the Filter button from within the Editing group on the Home tab (see page 91).

Hot tip

Filtering is turned on, and a filter icon (an arrow) is added to each heading, with an initial setting of Showing All.

2 Click a filter icon, e.g. on Continent, to display its AutoFilter

3 Click the Select All box, to deselect all entries, then select the specific entry you want, e.g. Oceania

4 Click OK to apply the filter

Number Filters

Don't forget

You can set number filters, where you specify a level at which to accept or reject entries, or choose an option such as accepting the top ten entries.

1 Display the AutoFilter for "Population" and choose all entries greater than 100,000

2 The filter icons for modified AutoFilters are changed to show that filtering is in effect for those particular columns

Beware

If you click the Filter button on the Data tab or the Home tab, it will remove all the filters and delete all the filter settings.

3 Click a filter icon and select the Clear Filter option to remove the filter for a particular column

4 The filter icon for that column reverts to an arrow, and the Showing All option will be applied

Select Specific Data

Suppose you want to examine the population values for the larger countries. You can hide away the information that's not relevant for that purpose:

Hot tip

Filter the rows and hide selected columns to remove from view the data not needed at the moment.

1 Use the AutoFilter on the "Population" column to display only countries whose populations are greater than 150 million

2 Click column A, press Ctrl, click columns C, D etc. and select Home, Format, Hide & Unhide, Hide Columns

3 The display will be restricted to the required data

This places the country names adjacent to the surface area and population values, ready for further analysis.

Don't forget

Sort the information if required, for example in descending order of population size.

Create a Chart

1 Highlight the data (including headers), then select the Insert tab and click the arrow on the Charts group

96

Hot tip

When you've created a chart, the Chart Tools Design, Layout and Format tabs are displayed, and you can select the Change Chart Type button to try one of the other options.

2 Choose the chart type and subtype, in this case Column and Clustered Column

Beware

The "Surface Area" values are numerically much smaller than the "Population" values, so they are very close to the horizontal axis, as you'll find if you click that axis adjacent to the "Population" bars. However, you can choose a secondary axis for the population values.

3 Click one of the "Population" columns and select Format Data Series

4 Choose Plot Series On Secondary Axis, and adjust Gap Width to 400%

Hot tip

By default, one data series would overlay the other, but adjusting the width for one of them allows you to view both sets of data together.

97

5 Use the Format tab to provide titles for the chart and the axes and to adjust the position of the legend

Don't forget

Select the Move Chart button on the Design tab to place the chart on a separate worksheet.

Import a List

The "Country" worksheet discussed previously includes the "Capital" column, which provides a link to a list of cities. If this list is available as a text file, you can import it into the worksheet.

 1 Select a cell marking the start of an empty section of the worksheet, and select the Data tab

2 Click Get External Data and choose From Text

3 Locate the text file and select Import, then follow the steps of the Text Import Wizard (see page 88)

City
Text Document
183 KB

Don't forget

There's a workbook open, so Excel offers you the choice of placing the data in the existing worksheet or in a new worksheet.

4 Click OK to place the data in the current worksheet, at the location selected initially

Create a Table

1 Click a cell within the data range and select the Insert tab, then click the Table button

2 Click Yes to confirm the range and accept the headers

3 The table will be created (using the default style)

Add Totals to Table

Hot tip

Convert the range of country data into table form, then add totals.

1 Click a cell within the country data, and select Insert, Table, then rename the new table as "Country"

2 Select the Table Tools Design tab, click the box for Total Row, then scroll to the bottom (press End then down)

Don't forget

The functions that you choose are entered as subfunctions of Subset, for example:

101	Average
102	Count numbers
103	Count
104	Max
105	Min
109	Sum

3 Select the Total box for "Name", click the arrow and choose the function, e.g. Count

4 Select the Sum function for columns with numerical values, such as "SurfaceArea", "Population" or "GNP"

You do not use the column and row labels to specify cells and ranges, you use the header name for the column (enclosed in square brackets).

	A	B	C	D	E	F
1	CountryCode	Name	Continent	Region	SurfaceArea	IndepYear
238	YUG	Yugoslavia	Europe	Southern Europe	102173	1918
239	ZMB	Zambia	Africa	Eastern Africa	752618	1964
240	ZWE	Zimbabwe	Africa	Eastern Africa	390757	1980
241	Total		239		148956306.9	

E241 = =SUBTOTAL(109,[SurfaceArea])

5 You can combine functions such as Min and Max, to show the range of values contained in a column such as "IndepYear"

 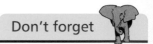

The headers contain AutoFilter icons, so you can limit the display to a section of the table.

F241 = =CONCATENATE("From ",SUBTOTAL(105,[IndepYear])," to ",SUBTOTAL(104,[IndepYear]))

	A	B	C	D	E	F
1	CountryCode	Name	Continent	Region	SurfaceArea	IndepYear
238	YUG	Yugoslavia	Europe	Southern Europe	102173	1918
239	ZMB	Zambia	Africa	Eastern Africa	752618	1964
240	ZWE	Zimbabwe	Africa	Eastern Africa	390757	1980
241	Total		239		148956306.9	From -1523 to 1994

6 When a column contains a set of discrete values, such as "Continent" or "Region", you can calculate the number of unique values that it contains

You can use any Excel function in the total boxes, not just the Subtotal function.

C241 = {=SUM(1/COUNTIF([Continent],[Continent]))}

	A	B	C	D	E	F
1	CountryCode	Name	Continent	Region	SurfaceArea	IndepYear
238	YUG	Yugoslavia	Europe	Southern Europe	102173	1918
239	ZMB	Zambia	Africa	Eastern Africa	752618	1964
240	ZWE	Zimbabwe	Africa	Eastern Africa	390757	1980
241	Total		239	7	25	148956306.9 From -1523 to 1994

This counts the number of times each individual value in the column is repeated, and uses these repeats to build up a count of the number of distinct values.

Computed Column

You can insert a column in the table without affecting other ranges or data or tables in the worksheet.

1 Click in the "Population" column, select the Home tab, click Insert, and choose Insert Table Columns to the Left

2 The new column is inserted and initially named Column1

3 Type a new name, such as "Density", and press Enter

4 Click in the first cell of the column, and type "=", then click the "Population" cell in the same row

The cell that you select is referenced as:
[#ThisRow],[Population]

5 Type "/", then click the "SurfaceArea" cell in the same row

Hot tip

The next cell that you select is referenced as:
[#ThisRow],[SurfaceArea]

6 Press Enter, and the expression is evaluated and copied to all the other cells in the table column

	B	C	D	E	F
1	Name	Continent	Region	SurfaceArea	IndepYear
2	Afghanistan	Asia	Southern and Centra	652090	1919
3	Albania	Europe	Southern Europe	28748	1912
4	Algeria	Africa	Northern Africa	2381741	1962
5	American Samoa	Oceania	Polynesia	199	
6	Andorra	Europe	Southern Europe	468	1278
7	Angola	Africa	Central Africa	1246700	1975
8	Anguilla	North America	Caribbean	96	
9	Antarctica	Antarctica	Antarctica	13120000	
10	Antigua and Barbu	North America	Caribbean	442	1981
11	Argentina	South America	South America	2780400	1816
12	Armenia	Asia	Middle East	29800	1991
13	Aruba	North America	Caribbean	193	
14	Australia	Oceania	Australia and New Z	7741220	1901
15	Austria	Europe	Western Europe	83859	1918
16	Azerbaijan	Asia	Middle East	86600	1991
17	Bahamas	North America	Caribbean	13878	1973
18	Bahrain	Asia	Middle East	694	1971

Don't forget

The result is the population density, the number of people per square kilometer.

Don't forget

The formula in each cell references [#ThisRow], which is the current row for that cell.

Table Lookup

The "Country" table contains a city code number for the capital city of each country, rather than the actual name.

The names are stored in the separate "City" table, which has details of more than 4000 cities.

To display the name of the capital city alongside the city number in the "Country" table:

1 Insert a table column next to the "Capital" column, and change its name to "CapitalCity"

2 In the first cell of this column type the expression "=VLOOKUP("

3 Click the adjacent cell in the "Capital" column, then type ",City,2,0)"

Hot tip

The table reference [#ThisRow],[Capital] is the "Capital" number from the current row. The other parameters are "City" (the table name), 2 (the column with the actual name) and 0 (the code for Exact Match).

4 Press Enter, and the capital-city name is inserted, on all the rows in the "Country" table, not just the current row

5 Scroll down to check the entries for particular countries, for example the United States (Washington) or the United Kingdom (London)

Beware

If the area does not have a capital city (e.g. United States Minor Outlying Islands) then the value #N/A is entered, to show no match found.

Manage Data Using Access

If you have large amounts of data or complex functions to handle, you may require the more comprehensive facilities in Access 2007.

Hot tip

You'll find Access 2007 in the Professional, Enterprise or Ultimate editions of Office 2007.

Microsoft Office Access 2007

1 Start Access from the Office folder on the Start menu and you'll be greeted by a range of database templates

Don't forget

Access uses the Office 2007 Fluent user interface (Ribbon technology), and can share data with other Office applications such as Excel, Word and PowerPoint.

2 Select a suitable template, for example Assets, change the suggested name if desired and click the Download button

3 Your copy of Office is validated, the selected template is downloaded and a new database is opened within Access

Hot tip

Access automatically displays a Help window, which offers advice on modifying and using your new database.

Security Within Access

 1 Click the Options button on the Security Warning

Don't forget

The database created is a complete tracking application with predefined tables, forms, reports, queries, macros, and relationships, ready for use immediately.

2 This tells you that Access has disabled the VBA macros included in the template (the default security option)

Microsoft Office Security Options

🛡 **Security Alert**

VBA Macro

Access has disabled potentially harmful content in this database.

If you trust the contents of this database and would like to enable it for this session only, click Enable this content.

Warning: It is not possible to determine that this content came from a trustworthy source. You should leave this content disabled unless the content provides critical functionality and you trust its source.

More information

File Path: C:\Users\Michael\Documents\Assets.accdb

◉ Help protect me from unknown content (recommended)

○ Enable this content

Open the Trust Center   OK   Cancel

 3 Click "Enable this content" (for the current session only)

○ Help protect me from unknown content (recommended)
◉ Enable this content

Beware

Do not enable macros in databases that you download, unless you are sure that the source of the file is trustworthy.

4 Click the Shutter Bar Open/Close button to display the list of database objects (tables and reports etc.)

Add Records

1 Click the New Asset button to add an entry to the Assets database

📧 New Asset

2 Enter the details for the item, selecting from a list of values on fields with an arrow, e.g. Category

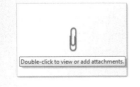
3 If the value you want is not listed, just right-click the box and select Edit List Items

4 Add or change entries as required and click OK

5 Click Save and New to save the current record and begin the record for a new asset

6 Presentations

Build a presentation, slide by slide, apply themes to create a consistent effect, and use animation to focus attention on particular points. Use a second monitor for a presenter view. Take advantage of templates, built in or downloaded, and print handouts for the presentation. Rehearse the show to get timings and create an automatic show.

Start a Presentation

Like Word, Excel and Access, the PowerPoint application uses the Office Fluent user interface (Ribbon technology), and displays tabs appropriate to the current activity.

To start PowerPoint and create a new presentation:

1 Select Start, All Programs, Microsoft Office and click the PowerPoint entry

2 Click to add a title as suggested, and type the title for the slide show, for example "Dickens World"

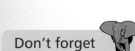
3 Click to add a subtitle, the second option, and type, e.g. "Themed Park, Chatham Maritime, Kent, UK" (the childhood home of Charles Dickens)

4 Select the Home tab and click the New Slide button in the Slides group

5 An empty title and content slide is added to the slide show

Hot tip

The new slide has option buttons to insert a table, chart, SmartArt graphic, picture from a file, clip art or media clip. See page 113 for an example.

111

6 Click on the prompts and add a title "Features of Dickens World" and bullet points to give the details

Don't forget

Click within a bullet item and press Shift+Tab to move it up (promote it) to the next level.

7 Press Enter to add a new bullet item, and the Tab key to move to the next lower level of bullet items

Expand the Slide

1 Continue to add items and you'll see the text size and spacing adjusted to fit the text onto the slide

112

Don't forget

Alternatively, you can choose to stop fitting text to the placeholder, to continue on a new slide, or to change to a two-column format.

2 Click the AutoFit Options button and select the option to Split Text Between Two Slides

Hot tip

The text size and spacing will be adjusted to take advantage of the extra space available.

3 A new slide is inserted, with the same layout and title as the original slide, and the bullet items are shared evenly between the two slides

Insert a Picture

1 Select the Home tab and click the arrow on the New Slide button in the Slides group to display the options

2 Choose a slide layout such as Picture with Caption

3 Click the icon to add a picture, as suggested in the prompt

Hot tip

There are nine standard layouts for slides, so you can select the one that's most appropriate for the specific content planned for each slide.

4 Locate and select the image file and click Insert, then "Click to add title", and "Click to add text"

Don't forget

The title and the text that you add provide the caption for the inserted image.

Apply a Theme

The default slides have a plain background, but you can choose a more effective theme and apply it to all the slides you've created.

Hot tip

The selected theme is temporarily applied to the current slide, to help you choose the most effective theme.

1 Select the Design tab, and move the mouse pointer over each of the themes to see the effect

Beware

To avoid losing your results, make sure to save the presentation periodically. Click the Save icon on the Quick Access toolbar or press the Ctrl+S shortcut key.

2 Click the preferred theme to apply it to all of the slides in the presentation

Don't forget

You can right-click your selected theme and choose to apply the theme to selected slides, or set the theme as the default for future slides.

Apply to All Slides
Apply to Selected Slides
Set as Default Theme
Add Gallery to Quick Access Toolbar

3 You can scroll the list to display additional themes, change the colors, fonts and effects for the current theme, and modify the type of background style it uses

To select the transition effects between slides:

1 Select the Animations tab and review the options – Wipes, Push and Cover, Stripes and Bars, Random

2 Click the up and down arrows to view another row of effects, or click the More button to see the full list

3 Click an effect to assign it to the current slide only, or click the button labelled Apply To All

By default, each slide advances to the next slide when you press the mouse key, but you can adjust the setting for individual slides.

4 Clear the On Mouse Click box to disable the mouse-key option for the current slide

5 Select the current slide to advance Automatically After a specified number of minutes and seconds

Whatever the setting, you can always advance the slide show by pressing one of the keyboard shortcuts, such as N (next), Enter, Page Down, right arrow or spacebar. To go back a step, you'd press P (previous), Page Up, left arrow, up arrow or Backspace.

Animations

You can apply animation effects to individual parts of a slide.

1 Select the Animations tab, pick a slide with bullet items and note that the Animate button is grayed (inactive)

2 Select the text box with the bullet items, and the Animate button is activated

3 Click the down arrow on the Animate box and choose, for example, Fly In, By 1st Level Paragraph, then click the Preview button to observe the effect

Run the Show

When you've added all the slides you need, you can try running the complete show to see the overall effect.

 1 Select the Slide Show tab and click the From the Beginning button in the Start Slide Show group

2 The slides are displayed full-screen, with the transition and animation effects that you selected

3 Click the final screen to terminate the slide show

Hot tip

You can also press F5 to run the slide show from the beginning, press Shift+F5 to run from the current slide, and press Esc to terminate.

Don't forget

You may need to use the mouse key or the keyboard shortcuts to go to the next slide or animation, if you haven't specified time limits for advancing slides.

117

Hot tip

When the slide show finishes, a black screen is presented, with the message: "End of slide show, click to exit."

End of slide show, click to exit.

Other Views

1 Select the View tab and select Slide Sorter to display all the slides so that you can rearrange their sequence

2 Select the Notes Page view to see the current slide with its notes (information and prompts for the presenter)

3 Click the Zoom button and select a zoom level to examine parts of the slide or the notes, then click OK

4 Select Fit and click OK, or click the Fit to Window button, to resize the view to make the whole page visible

5 You can also drag the slider on the zoom bar to change the size

6 To switch back to the view with slide bar and current slide, click the Normal button

The view you select will be retained when you select another tab, so you should revert to the required view before leaving.

7 To reveal more of the notes area, click and drag the separator bar

8 Click the Outline tab to see the text contents of the slides, giving a summary view of the presentation, then click the Slides tab to redisplay the slides bar

Hot tip

The buttons next to the Zoom bar provide the Normal, Slide Sorter and Slide Show views

Presenter View

Hot tip

If your system has dual-monitor support, you can run your presentation from one monitor while your audience views it on a second monitor (or on a projector screen).

Don't forget

You can also right-click the desktop, select the Personalize option and then select Display Settings.

1 Select the Slide Show tab and click the box to enable the Use Presenter View option

2 If you do not have a second monitor enabled, you'll be warned that this a requirement for Presenter View

3 Click Check, and the Display Settings panel is opened

4 Select the second monitor and extend the desktop

5 Click Yes to keep these settings

6 With dual-monitor support enabled, you will be able to select the Use Presenter View option

7 Select the View tab and click the Slide Show button to run the presentation on two monitors

121

Use a Template

1 To review your templates, click the Office button, then click New and select a category, e.g. Installed Templates

2 Select a template, for example Widescreen Presentation, and click the Create button to see the contents

3 Select the View tab and click Slide Sorter to get an overview, or click Slide Show to see the presentation

4 Presentations you create from templates will be saved only when you explicitly select the Save command

Open one of the Photo Album templates:

1 Select the Office button, click New, Installed Templates, select Contemporary Photo Album and click Create

2 This displays sample pages to help you get started

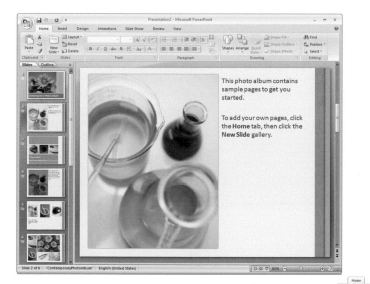

3 Select the Home tab and click the New Slide button to review more than 20 different arrangements of photos and captions, to choose the layout most suited to the specific pictures you want to display

Don't forget

There is tailored support in PowerPoint for photos, as illustrated by the Photo Album templates.

Don't forget

You can replace any of the example photos with your own pictures, and edit the text to provide your own captions.

123

Hot tip

The Classic photo album contains a similar set of page layouts, but uses rather more sedate black-and-white images to illustrate the options.

Download a Template

You can download templates from Microsoft Office Online

1 Select the Office button, click New and choose one of the Microsoft Office Online categories

2 For example, Content Slides offers individual slides that can be downloaded and inserted into your presentations

3 Select "More categories", "Name and place cards", then select and download the Numbered Table Tents template

4 Follow the instructions in the notes, to print and prepare the table place tags, making changes to the text as needed

Print the Slide Show

1 Click the Office button, then click the Print button to specify the printer and other printing options

Hot tip

Click the arrow next to the Print button and select Print Preview, to check what will be printed. Select Quick Print to get an immediate print when no changes to printing options are needed.

2 Select the printer and the print range (slides required, by number)

3 Choose what type of document to print

Don't forget

You can choose to print the document in grayscale or pure black-and-white, even if the presentation itself is in full color.

Color
Grayscale
Pure Black and White

4 If you select Handouts, additional options will be enabled

Hot tip

Click the Preview button to see the effect of your selected printing options.

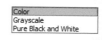

5 Specify the number of slides to a page, and the order (horizontal or vertical). You can also select Scale to Fit Paper, Frames Slides and High Quality

Rehearse Timings

To establish the timings for each slide, you need to rehearse the presentation and record the times for each step.

1 Select the Slide Show tab and click Rehearse Timings, which is in the Set Up group

2 The slide show runs full-screen in manual mode, with the timer superimposed at the top left corner

3 Advance each slide or animation, allowing for viewing and narration etc., and the times will be recorded

4 When the presentation finishes you can choose to keep the new slide timings for use next time you view the show

Microsoft Office PowerPoint

The total time for the slide show was 0:00:59. Do you want to keep the new slide timings to use when you view the slide show?

Yes   No

5 The view changes to Slide Sorter, with individual times for the slides, and Use Rehearsed Timings is selected

Save As Options

There are several forms in which you can save your presentation.

 1   Select the Office button and click the arrow next to the Save As button

2   PowerPoint Presentation is the default and saves the presentation in a form that can be changed and updated

3   Select PowerPoint Show to save in a form that cannot be modified and automatically opens in the Slide Show view

4   To see what other formats are supported, click the Save As button, then click the down arrow for "Save as type"

Package for CD

Hot tip

You can save the presentation to a CD or folder and view it on systems that have no version of PowerPoint.

1 With the required presentation open, select the Office button, click the Publish button and select the Package for CD option

Distribute the document to other people

Package for CD
Copy the presentation and media links to a folder that can be burned to a CD.

Publish Slides
Save slides to a Slide Library or other location to reuse later.

Create Handouts in Microsoft Office Word
Open the presentation in Word and prepare custom handout pages.

Document Management Server
Share the presentation by saving it to a document management server.

Create Document Workspace
Create a new site for the presentation and keep the local copy synchronized.

Package for CD

Copy presentations to a CD that will play on computers running Microsoft Windows 2000 or later, even without PowerPoint.

Name the CD: PresentationCD

Files to be copied:

Dickens World.ppt   Add Files...

Linked files and the PowerPoint Viewer are included by default. To change this, click Options.   Options...

Copy to Folder...   Copy to CD   Close

Don't forget

Click Add to include additional presentations in the package, and specify in which order to run them.

Package for CD

Copy presentations to a CD that will play on computers running Microsoft Windows 2000 or later, even without PowerPoint.

Name the CD: Dickens World

Play order Files to be copied
1 Dickens World.ppt   Add...
2 Dickens.ppt   Remove

Options...

Linked files and the PowerPoint Viewer are included by default. To change this, click Options.

Copy to Folder...   Copy to CD   Close

2 Type a name for the package and click Copy to Folder

Package for CD

Copy presentations to a CD that will play on computers running Microsoft Windows 2000 or later, even without PowerPoint.

Name the CD: Dickens World

Files to be copied:

Dickens World.ppt   Add Files...

Linked files and the PowerPoint Viewer are included by default. To change this, click Options.   Options...

Copy to Folder...   Copy to CD   Close

3 Edit the folder name and location if necessary, then click OK

Copy to Folder

Copy files to a new folder with a name and location you specify.

Folder name: Dickens World

Location: C:\Users\Michael\Documents\   Browse...

OK   Cancel

4 The presentation files are added, along with all the files needed to run the PowerPoint Viewer

7 Office Extras

There are many extras included with all editions of Office, including Picture Manager for editing images, Document Imaging with its OCR capability, and Clip Organizer to manage media files on your computer. There are more tools and facilities available from the Office download websites.

Office Tools

The Office suite includes a set of tools, as well as applications. Not all the tools will be available, but you can run Office setup to add the ones you want.

Although the option is called Uninstall, it also provides facilities to change or repair programs.

To see which tools are already installed on your system:

1 Select Start, All Programs, Microsoft Office, Microsoft Office Tools for a list

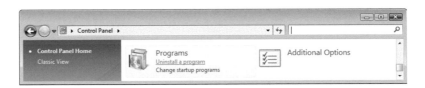

2 To look for more tools, select Start, Control Panel and click the link Uninstall a Program

3 Select Microsoft Office 2007 and click Change

4 Select Add or Remove Features and click Continue

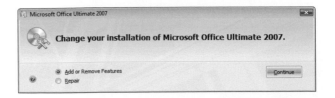

5 Scroll to Office Tools, click [+] to expand the list, click an entry heading and select Run from My Computer

Hot tip

Click a group heading (with [+] or [–]) and choose Run All from My Computer, to add all the tools in that group.

Don't forget

There are also tools in the Shared Features section, which may be selected for installation.

131

6 When you've selected all that you want, click Continue and the programs will be copied and configured for use

7 Click Close to finish setup when configuration finishes

8 New entries will be added to the Microsoft Office Tools folder in the Start Menu

Picture Manager

This tool helps you manage, edit and share your pictures, wherever they are located. It can also provide automatic corrections and adjustments such as red-eye removal.

Picture Manager displays the Shortcuts pane and Task pane, as well as the Preview pane. Use the View command to turn these off (see page 133).

1 Select Microsoft Office Picture Manager from the Microsoft Office Tools folder in the Start menu

2 Picture Manager shows the image-file contents of your Pictures folder in the Preview pane

Don't forget

If the folder you select contains no picture files, you'll get an appropriate message. For example, when you select Photos:

3 Click the [+] to expand the folder list and select a folder from within Pictures, e.g. "Photos\Vancouver"

Hot tip

Click the arrow on the Zoom button to select a specific zoom factor, such as 50% of the usual thumbnail size (or of the full picture size in the other views).

4 Drag the Zoom-bar slider to shrink the thumbnails and display more images at a time, or enlarge the thumbnails to display larger (but fewer) images

132

5 Click Filmstrip View on the Views toolbar

Hot tip

You can change the style of the display in the Preview pane, using the Views toolbar.

6 Click Single Picture View on the Views toolbar

Hot tip

The zoom factor in these views is the size of the main image relative to the full picture size.

133

7 To close the Shortcuts and Task panes, click the View command and select the appropriate entry to toggle the setting (or click the [x] at the top right of the Shortcuts or Task pane)

Don't forget

The View command also allows you to choose the Preview style and whether to display file names or non-picture-file types.

Edit Pictures

You can adjust the brightness, contrast and color of your pictures, apply red-eye removal, or crop, resize, rotate and flip.

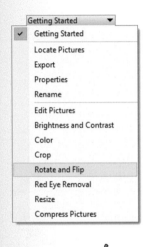
1 Click the Picture command on the menu bar and select the function you require, e.g. Rotate and Flip

2 Select the picture or pictures that you want to change

3 Select the subfunction, e.g. "Rotate right" (default 90°)

4 Right–click Unsaved Edits and select Save All (or Discard All)

Add Picture Shortcuts

If you have picture files in other folders on your hard disk or on your network, you can add shortcuts to give you quick access without having to navigate the full path.

 Select Add Picture Shortcut (on Shortcuts pane) or "Add a new picture shortcut" (on Getting Started Task pane)

 Navigate to the folder that you require and click Add

 A shortcut to the selected folder will be inserted

Hot tip

Select "Locate pictures" in Getting Started, to search for folders on your system that contain picture files and add them as shortcuts.

135

Don't forget

You can select folders on any drive on your computer or another computer on the same network (as long as you have authorization to share files and folders).

Don't forget

You can add or remove folders, paste files or rename the shortcut, and all the changes will be reflected in the actual folder, whether it is on the hard disk or the network.

Document Imaging

With Document Imaging, you can scan both single- and multi-page documents and carry out optical character recognition (OCR). There's a separate Document Scanning component listed in the Start menu, though you perform all operations via the Document Imaging program. For example, to scan a document:

1 Select Document Imaging from Microsoft Office Tools in the Start menu and click Scan New Document

2 Check the settings, and make any appropriate changes, e.g. color, double-sided or multiple-page documents

3 Click the Scan button to initiate scanning of the documents

4 Click the Zoom button to see the document close up

OCR has already been carried out on the document, as you'll see if you click the Recognize Text Using OCR button.

5 Click the Send Text to Word button to see the OCR text

Don't forget

You can use Document Imaging to apply OCR to recognize text in any image document, not just scanned images.

Don't forget

The results of the OCR are displayed in .htm format, but you can save them in a standard Word document.

6 Save the document in .docx format if desired

Language Settings

You may need to work with documents in other languages.

 This document includes text in Welsh, which confuses the default English (United States) spelling checker

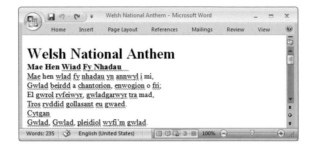

2 To check which languages are enabled and add a new language, click Office Language Settings in Office Tools

3 Select the language you require and click Add, and repeat this for each additional language

Clip Organizer

To make use of Clip Art in an Office application, e.g. PowerPoint:

 1 Select the Insert tab and click the Clip Art button (or click Clip Art on the Content bar shown on new slides)

This launches the Clip Art task pane, so you can search your clip-art collections. To help you build and manage these collections:

2 Select Start, All Programs, Microsoft Office, Microsoft Office Tools and then Microsoft Clip Organizer

3 Select Office Collections to explore the clip art included

Hot tip

Clip art includes vector images (computed lines and curves), which can be resized without loss of quality. They are used in Word, Excel, Outlook, PowerPoint and the non-Ribbon-style Publisher.

Don't forget

The Clip Organizer in the Office Tools folder provides a separate way of running the same software that's used in the Office applications to find and insert clip art.

139

Don't forget

The Office suite includes over 400 items of clip art, organized into around 40 categories and described by a series of keywords that can be used for searches.

Web Collections

The Web Collections include an entry for the Office clip-art collection available from Microsoft Office Online.

1 Select one of the categories to view the first 100 entries of the typically 1000+ items in each category

Don't forget

You can specify a collection, or choose individual categories within the collection.

You can also specify which media file types you are interested in.

2 Click the Search button, enter one or more keywords and the search characteristics and click the Go button

Hot tip

Select Make Available Offline, and choose one of your local collections to hold the copy.

3 Select an item, click the arrow that appears at the right, then select Preview/Properties to see the details, including a larger version

Catalog Your Media Files

To locate the media files on your system:

1 Select File, Add Clips to Organizer, Automatically

Don't forget

Clip Organizer can manage all the media files on your system, pictures and music as well as clip art.

2 Click OK and Clip Organizer will catalog all of the media files on your hard disks

Hot tip

Select Options to choose the specific folders to include in the search for media files.

141

3 You can now explore the collections that have been added

Don't forget

If there are entries you don't need, right-click them and select Delete. This deletes the Clip Organizer entry only, not the original folder.

Office Downloads

There are additional tools and facilities for Office at the Microsoft website. To find what's available for your system:

1 Go to www.microsoft.com and click the Downloads tab

2 Scroll down to the Browse Downloads by Product section

3 Click the link "Build your list" and then click the button "Autodetect your products"

4 The list is generated; you can select "Save your settings"

Don't forget

You will be asked to provide your Windows Live email address and password (or to register if you have not already done so).

5 The list shows all your applications that have downloads

6 Click an application, e.g. Word 2007, to see its downloads

Hot tip

The entries will be different for each application but may include items in the Add-ins, Audio, Converters, Demos, Publications, Tools, Updates and Viewers categories.

Get Started Tab

1 Click Add-ins in Word 2007 downloads (see page 143) and select the add-in Get Started Tab for Word 2007

2 Select Continue to validate your copy of Office

3 Select Download and follow the prompts to download and run the installation program for the add-in

4 The Get Started Tab Setup Wizard guides you through the steps to configure the application for the new function

5 When you next start the application, the Get Started tab appears, with its range of training resources

145

6 Click, for example, "Get up to Speed with Word 2007"

Office System Downloads

There are a number of non-application-specific downloads for the 2007 Office system that aren't shown on your customized product list.

Hot tip

When you move the mouse over a command or toolbar button, CLIP displays a translation in a tooltip or window. Translations between French, Alsatian and English are supported. You can also provide your own translations.

1 Display the Browse Downloads by Products section (see page 142) and click the 2007 Office System tab

2 Select "2007 Office system" to see download categories

3 Select Tools and download, for example, the Captions Language Interface Pack (CLIP), a translation aid

8 Email

The first time you use Outlook you may need to specify your email account. Then you can receive messages, save attachments, print messages, issue replies and update your address book, while protecting yourself from spam messages that might be targeted at your account. You can add a standard signature note to your messages. Outlook helps you subscribe to RSS feeds.

Starting Outlook

Both Windows and Microsoft Office provide email support. To see which is the default email program on your system:

Hot tip

If you are running a Windows XP system, you see similar entries, except that Outlook Express rather than Windows Mail is the alternative email option.

1 Select Start, and view the entries at the top of the menu

2 Where Microsoft Office Outlook appears as the E-mail option, click this to launch the program

3 Where Windows Mail is shown as the E-mail option, click All Programs and select Microsoft Office

Don't forget

This makes Outlook the default, then starts the application. In future you'll be able to select Outlook from the top of the Start menu (as shown in step 2).

4 Click Microsoft Office Outlook 2007, then click Yes

The first time you start Outlook, it takes you through the process of defining an email account.

 Choose to configure an email account and click Next

2 Type your name, your email address and your password

Configure Server Settings

Don't forget

Your connection to the Internet must be active at this time, so that the wizard can make the connection.

1 The wizard identifies your Internet connection and establishes the network connection

> Add New E-mail Account
>
> **Online search for your server settings...**
>
> **Configuring**
>
> Configuring e-mail server settings. This might take several minutes:
>
> ✓ Establish network connection
> ▸ **Search for michael.price33@btinternet.com server settings**
>   Log on to server
>
> < Back   Next >   Cancel

2 The wizard then searches for the server settings that support your email account

> Add New E-mail Account
>
> **Online search for your server settings...**
>
> **Configuring**
>
> Configuring e-mail server settings. This might take several minutes:
>
> ✓ Establish network connection
> ✓ Search for michael.price33@btinternet.com server settings
> ▸ **Log on to server and send a test e-mail message**
>
> < Back   Next >   Cancel

Hot tip

This illustrates the process for the POP3 email account, the standard type. You may need to select the manual configuration for other types of server, using the information provided by your email supplier.

3 Finally, the wizard logs on to the server using your account name and password and sends a test message

> Add New E-mail Account
>
> **Online search for your server settings...**
>
> **Configuring**
>
> Configuring e-mail server settings. This might take several minutes:
>
> ✓ Establish network connection
> ✓ Search for michael.price33@btinternet.com server settings
> ✓ Log on to server and send a test e-mail message
>
> Your **POP3** e-mail account is successfully configured.
>
> ☐ Manually configure server settings
>
> < Back   Finish   Cancel

4 Click Finish and your email account will be configured

Your First Messages

Outlook opens with the Inbox showing your first email messages, e.g. welcome messages from the ISP and an Outlook test message.

Hot tip

The main Outlook window uses the conventional menu-bar style. However, the Outlook editors use the Microsoft Fluent Ribbon technology for messages and tasks (see page 11).

Title bar   Menu bar   Standard toolbar   Search box   To-Do bar

Calendar

Appointment list

Task list

Navigation pane   Outlook View bars   Folders list   Folder pane   Reading pane

You may also receive messages from Outlook of a different type, related to setting up and configuration, for example:

1. Click Yes to synchronize your RSS feeds with the Common Feed List, or click Remind Me Later

2. Click Yes to transfer any existing email accounts from Windows Mail (or Outlook Express) to Outlook

The details for the existing email accounts will be added to the Outlook account settings.

Don't forget

This does not transfer messages from the previous email program. However, new messages will be downloaded to Outlook.

Turn Off Reading Pane

The currently-selected message is displayed in the Reading pane (as shown on page 151). This is a convenient way to scan messages, but has the drawback that messages will be opened even if they are potentially hazardous. To avoid this, you can turn off the reading pane.

(as shown on page 151)

Hot tip

It is possible that the very act of reading an email message could release harmful software into your system. Turning off the Reading pane allows you to review the message source and title before it is actually read.

1 Select View, Reading Pane and choose Off rather than Right or Bottom

2 Messages will now be left unread until you double-click (or select and press Enter) to open them

Don't forget

Messages are shown arranged by date and shown in groups. You can change the view, for example to sort by sender or subject. When you open a message, you can see that the message editor uses Ribbon-technology function and styling, though there's just a single Message tab in this View mode.

3 When the message has been opened, its entry in the Inbox folder is shown in regular rather than bold font

4 Click the Office button and select Close, or press Alt+F4 or click the Close button to end the display of the message

Request a Newsletter

You'll need to share your email address with friends, contacts and organizations to begin exchanging messages. You can also use your email address to request newsletters. For example:

1 Visit the website www.marshaperry.org/lists

2 Click on the hyperlink "Dickens"

3 Enter your email address, re-enter it to confirm and click Submit

4 Your email address is added to the list and an email inviting you to accept the subscription will be sent

5 Check your Inbox periodically for the message

Hot tip

www.marshaperry.org sponsors newsletters related to Charles Dickens and the Gad's Hill Place website at www.marshaperry.org/dickens.

153

Don't forget

There may be a fee in some cases, though most often newsletters are provided free of charge.

...cont'd

6 Double-click the message when it arrives in your Inbox

Your address could be provided, accidently or deliberately, without your permission, so you must explicitly confirm your wishes.

7 Select the link provided to confirm you issued the request

Retain this email, since it provides the links needed to change your details, or to unsubscribe if you no longer wish to receive the newsletter.

8 Another email will arrive, completing the subscription

Receive a Message

To check for any mail that may be waiting:

 1 Open Outlook, select the Inbox folder and click the Send/Receive button

2 New mail will be downloaded and displayed in the Inbox

Hot tip

Depending on the settings, Outlook may automatically issue a Send/Receive when it starts up.

[Screenshot of Inbox – Microsoft Outlook window showing the Inbox folder with messages including "Sue... Dickens Material Sun 7/15... 1 MB" and a To-Do Bar with July 2007 calendar]

155

3 Double-click the message title to display the contents

[Screenshot of "Dickens Material – Message (HTML)" window showing the message ribbon and the email from Sue Price with attachments Charles_Dickens_young.jpg (757 KB), Little_Nell_Journey.jpg (387 KB), and London Map.jpg (102 KB)]

From: Sue Price [sue.price25@btinternet.com]   Sent: Sun 7/15/2007 8:00 AM
To: michael.price33@btinternet.com
Cc:
Subject: Dickens Material

Hello Michael,
I came across some pictures that you might find useful for your Charles Dickens study. There's a map showing the probable route for Little Nell's journey from London to Tong. The second map is of Dickens London. I laso came across a pictures of the young Charles Dickens which might also come in useful. Finally, here's a link to the full text of The Old Curiosity Shop: http://www.gutenberg.org/dirs/etext96/curio10.txt
Let me know what else you migh find useful,
Regards,
Sue.

Don't forget

You can also save attachments directly from the Inbox folder, without opening the message (see page 156).

4 Click Other Actions in the Actions group and select Save Attachments, to transfer the attachments to your hard drive

Save Attachments

To save the attachments without opening the message:

1 Select the message, then click File and select Save Attachments, All Attachments

2 In either case, the list of attachments is displayed, so you can amend the selection

3 Press Ctrl and click a selected attachment to remove that item, then click OK to download

4 Locate the folder to receive the downloads (or click Organize to create a new folder), then click OK

5 The attachments will be added to the selected folder

Print the Message

1 Click the Office button, select the arrow next to the Print button, then click the Print option

2 You can change the printer or adjust the print settings, for example change the number of copies required

3 Click the "Print options" box to print the attached files as well as the message itself

4 For picture attachments, you can choose the print size (e.g. full page, 4″ × 6″ etc.)

Hot tip

Select Print Preview to see how the message will appear on the page. Select Quick Print to send the message to the printer using all the default settings.

Beware

Each attachment will print as a separate print job destined for the default printer. You can change the printer and the print size on each job, but you cannot combine the prints onto the same sheet.

Reply to the Message

1 When you want to reply to a message that you've just opened, click the Reply button in the Respond group on the Message tab

2 The message form opens with the email address and subject entered and the cursor in the message area, ready for you to type your comments above the original text

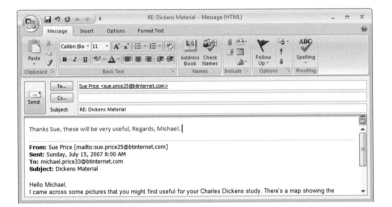

3 Complete your response and then click the Send button at the head of the message

Add Address to Contacts

Whenever you receive an email, you can add the sender (and any other addressees) to your Outlook Contacts list

Hot tip

You can record a large amount of information, personal or business, for the entries in your Contacts folder.

1 Right-click the email address and select Add to Outlook Contacts

2 Add any extra information you have and click Save & Close

3 Select the Outlook folder to create and update entries

Don't forget

Double-click an entry to open it and review or amend the details.

159

Spam and Phishing

As useful as email can be, it does have a couple of problem areas. Because email is so cheap and easy to use, the criminally inclined try to take advantage of it for their own profit. They'll send out thousands of spam (junk email) messages, in the hope of getting one or two replies.

The Junk E-mail filter in Outlook catches the most obvious spam, based on its structure and content and moves such messages to the Junk E-mail folder, giving you a warning message.

160

To adjust the settings that the filter uses:

1 Select Tools, Options then click the Junk E-mail button in Preferences

2 Select the level of protection: No Automatic Filtering, Low (the default), High or Safe Lists Only

Some spam messages try to trick you into providing details such as passwords, PINs, and validation code. These messages are referred to as phishing (pronounced "fishing"), and are disguised to look like they are from a well-known organization such as a bank, credit card company or charity.

 Links to pictures on the sender's website may be blocked

 Links to websites may be disabled, and you may not be allowed to use the Reply and Reply All functions

 Alternatively, the links may be intercepted in Internet Explorer, with an explanation and caution

Hot tip

The messages are addressed to "Dear valued customer" rather than to you personally, and imply urgency, so that you'll respond quickly, without thinking.

Beware

You can continue to the website, but this is not recommended unless you are absolutely sure that this is not a problem website.

Create a Message

1 Select the Mail folder and click the New button to open a new mail message form

2 Click the To button to open the address book, select the addressee and click To, then click OK

3 Type the subject, greeting and text for your message

Insert a Signature

You can create a standard signature to add to the emails you send.

1 Select the Insert tab and click Signature in the Include group to open the Signatures editor

2 Click the New button, specify a name for the new signature, then click OK

3 Add the text required and click OK to save the signature

4 Now click Signature again and select the new signature to insert it into the message, below the text. For example:

163

Hot tip

The first time you select the Signature button, there'll be no signatures defined, so you must start off by creating one.

Don't forget

You can specify one of your signatures as the default for new messages or for replies and forwards, and the appropriate signature will be automatically applied for future messages.

Don't forget

Click the Send button to store the message in the Outbox ready for sending.

Color Categories

You can use color to help sort and organize your messages.

Hot tip

Select the Minimize button to minimize the Navigation pane or the To-Do bar, to make more space for the message properties.

To associate a color with a message:

1 Select the message, click the Categorize button on the toolbar and choose the applicable color

2 The first time you select a specific color, you'll be asked if you want to rename it or assign a shortcut key

Don't forget

Choose Set Quick Click to define the color category to be assigned when you single-click the Categories column.

3 Select the All Categories entry to assign more than one color category to a message, or to add, rename or delete the color categories used

RSS Feeds

RSS (Really Simple Syndication) is a way for publishers of Internet data to make news, blogs and other information available to subscribers. You can add feeds and view subscriptions in either Internet Explorer or Outlook. To keep these programs in step:

 When prompted, click Yes to synchronize Outlook's list with the Common Feed List

2. Click RSS Feeds in Personal Folders for an overview

3. Scroll down to view featured RSS feeds and Office feeds

4 When you select a new feed, you must confirm that you want a subscription

5 The subscription will be enabled, and the recent history will be downloaded in a subfolder for that feed

To add an RSS feed for which you have been given the URL:

1 Select Tools, Account Settings, click the RSS Feeds tab and select New

2 Type the URL for the RSS feed you require and click Add to subscribe and insert it into the RSS Feeds folder

9 Time Management

Outlook is much more than an email manager. It is a complete personal information management system with full diary and calendar facilities. It enables you to keep track of appointments and meetings, and to control and schedule your tasks. You can keep notes, make journal entries and correlate all these with the email messages related to those records.

Outlook Calendar

The Outlook Calendar handles time-based activities including appointments, meetings, holidays, courses and events (single-day or multi-day activities). It provides a high-level view by day, week or month and will give you reminders when an activity, a meeting, or an anniversary perhaps, is due to happen. To open:

1 Click the Calendar button on the Navigation pane

Date navigator   Time bar   View   Events   Meeting

Calendar button   Appointments   Task

You can also view current calendar events on the Today page:

1 Select the Mail button and click Personal Folders

Schedule an Appointment

An appointment reserves space in your calendar for an activity that does not involve inviting other people or reserving resources.

1 Open the Calendar (day, week or month view) and use the date navigator to select the day for the appointment

2 Move the mouse pointer over the time when the appointment should begin, then click as prompted

3 Type the subject, then drag the handle on the lower edge to extend the appointment to the required duration

Hot tip

If the large Calendar button is hidden, click the small calendar button on the folder bar at the foot of the Navigation pane.

Don't forget

You drag the handle on the top edge to adjust the starting time for the appointment.

Change Appointment Details

You can change and add to the information stored in the calendar.

1 Double-click the appointment to open the appointment editor form showing the information provided so far

2 Add or change details such as the start time, end time, location or description as needed, then click Save & Close

3 The appointment is displayed in your calendar, alongside any other entries for that time of day

Recurring Appointments

When you have an activity that's repeated on a regular basis, you can define it as a recurring appointment.

 1 Open the appointments form and specify the details for a first occurrence of the activity, then click Recurrence

Hot tip

You can take an existing appointment or meeting, and click Recurrence to make it a recurring activity.

2 Specify how often the activity will be repeated, and over what range of time it should take place

3 Click OK and then click Save & Close to record the changes

Beware

Unless you limit the number of recurrences or set a termination date, the activity will be scheduled for all possible days in the future.

Don't forget

All the occurrences of the activity will now be displayed in the calendar on the appropriate days. If there's room, the recurrence symbol will appear after the subject.

Create a Meeting

1 Double-click the appointment entry in the calendar and click the Invite Attendees button in the Actions group

2 On the invitation message form displayed, click the To button to open the address book

3 Select the email address for each attendee in turn, and click the Required or the Optional button, then click OK

4 When all the attendees have been added, click the Send button to send the invitation to each of them

5 The invitation will be received as a normal email message

6 The meeting organizer is not required to respond

Beware

The attendees must be using a version of Outlook in order to be able to properly receive and respond to invitations.

173

Respond to an Invitation

1 When other attendees receive and open the invitation, it provides buttons to accept, decline or propose a new time

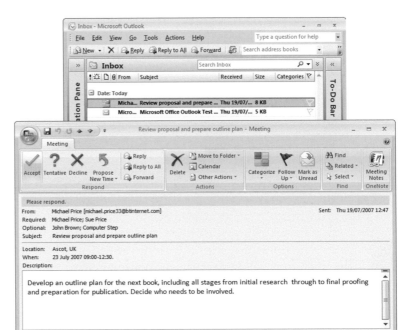

2 Click Accept, then OK, to send your response and add the appointment to your calendar

3 The original message is removed from the Inbox and the response is inserted into the Sent box

4 The originator will receive the responses from attendees as email messages in the Inbox

Don't forget

The message shows the current status, so it will show the latest information each time it is opened.

175

5 The message shows the attendee's response and the status

6 The meeting record displays the updated status

Hot tip

Any changes that the originator makes to the meeting details will be sent as update messages to the attendees.

Report Free/Busy Time

Outlook can help you choose the most suitable times to hold meetings, based on reports from the proposed attendees, giving details of their availability.

To publish this information, each attendee should:

1 Open Outlook and from the menu bar select Tools, Options

2 In the Calendar section on the Preferences tab, click the Calendar Options button

3 In the "Advanced options" section of Calendar Options, click the Free/Busy Options button

4 Click the box labelled "Publish at my location"

Hot tip

You can specify how much information to provide, and how often to issue updates. In the example, details will be published covering the next two months, and updates will be recorded once an hour.

5 Provide the path to the shared location, in this example the Shared Documents folder on a networked computer

6 For potential meeting originators only, put the same path, but "%NAMES%" as the username to search for any user

7 Click OK to initiate the reporting

The files will be stored in the specified location. They will be updated at the specified frequency. To create an immediate update, following major calendar changes for example:

Don't forget

The free/busy data is stored in a .vfb file with the file name the same as the username section of your email account.

1 From the menu bar select Tools, Send/Receive and then click the Free/Busy Information entry

2 The file is updated and a message will be displayed

Schedule a Meeting

You can use the reported free/busy information to help set up a meeting. For example, to reschedule a meeting you've just set up:

1 Open the meeting details and click the Scheduling button

178

2 Click AutoPick Next to see the next available time slot

3 Click Send to update the meeting and send a message to all attendees showing the changes that have been made and requesting a response

Add Holidays

To make sure that your calendar is an accurate reflection of your availability, add details of national holidays and similar events.

1 Select Tools, Options, Calendar Options (see page 176), then click the Add Holidays button

Calendar Options...

Add Holidays...

2 Select the countries that you wish to add

3 Click OK to insert the holidays and events for the selected countries

Add Holidays to Calendar

Select the locations whose holidays you would like copied to your Outlook Calendar:

- Thailand
- Tunisia
- Turkey
- Ukraine
- United Arab Emirates
- United Kingdom
- ☑ United States
- Uruguay
- Venezuela
- Yemen

OK   Cancel

Microsoft Office Outlook

The holidays were added to your Calendar.

OK

4 Click OK to exit

View

Arrange By ▶
Current View ▶
AutoPreview
Expand/Collapse Groups ▶
Navigation Pane ▶
To-Do Bar ▶
Reading Pane ▶
Reminders Window
Toolbars ▶
Status Bar
Refresh   F5

Day/Week/Month
Day/Week/Month View With AutoPreview
All Appointments
Active Appointments
✓ Events
Annual Events
Recurring Appointments
By Category
Outlook Data Files
Customize Current View...
Define Views...
Format Columns...

5 To see the new entries that have been added, select View, Current View, Events

Hot tip

By default, no holidays or special events are shown in your Calendar, but Outlook has a holiday file with information for 88 countries and events for the years 2006–2012.

Don't forget

Your own country or region is automatically selected the first time you choose the Add Holidays option.

179

Calendar - Microsoft Outlook

File   Edit   View   Go   Tools   Actions   Help   Type a question for help

New ▾ | 🖶 ✕ | 🔳 🔲 | Search address books   ▾ | ⑳ ▾

Calendar		(Filter Applied)	Search Calendar			⌕ ▾ ▾
🗋 🖉 Subject		Location	Recurrence Ra...	Durati...	Recur...	Categories
Recurrence: (none) (174 items)						
New Year's Day		United States	Sun 1/1/2006	1 day		Holiday
Martin Luther King Day		United States	Mon 1/16/2006	1 day		Holiday
Groundhog Day		United States	Thu 2/2/2006	1 day		Holiday
Lincoln's Birthday		United States	Sun 2/12/2006	1 day		Holiday
Valentine's Day		United States	Tue 2/14/2006	1 day		Holiday
Presidents' Day		United States	Mon 2/20/2006	1 day		Holiday
Saint Patrick's Day		United States	Fri 3/17/2006	1 day		Holiday
Easter Day		United States	Sun 4/16/2006	1 day		Holiday
Tax Day		United States	Mon 4/17/2006	1 day		Holiday
Administrative Professionals Day		United States	Wed 4/26/2006	1 day		Holiday

Calendar

All Calendar Items
My Calendars

How to Share Calendars
Search Calendars Online
Send a Calendar via E-mail...
Publish My Calendar...
Add New Group

Filter Applied   185 Items

Hot tip

If you have more than one country inserted, you can click Location to sort the events into country groupings. Use this, for example, to remove events for one country.

Creating Tasks

To create an implicit task:

Hot tip

Outlook can create and manage implicit tasks, which are follow-ups of other Outlook items. It can also create explicit tasks, which can be assigned to others.

1 Right-click an Outlook item (for example a message or contact), select Follow Up and select the flag for the timing

2 The follow-up item is added to the Task folder and also appears on the To-Do bar

To create an explicit task:

1 Click the prompt "Type a new task", in the Task folder or on the To-Do bar

Don't forget

This provides a quick way to generate a To-Do list of actions. Note that entries change color to red when the due date has passed.

2 Type the subject for the task and press Enter

3 The task is inserted with the default characteristics (current date for the start and the due date, and no reminder time)

...cont'd

To make changes to the details for the task:

1 Double-click the task entry in the To-Do bar or Task folder

2 You can change the start date or the due date, add a description, apply a reminder, update the priority or indicate how much has been completed

3 To update the status, click the down arrow and select the appropriate entry from the list

4 Click the Details button in the Show group to add secondary information related to the cost and expense of carrying out the task

Don't forget

As with the editors for other Outlook items, the Task editor uses the Ribbon technology.

Hot tip

Click the arrows on the "% Complete" box to increase or decrease by 25% at a time, or type an exact percentage in the box.

181

Don't forget

Click Save & Close, in Task or Details view, to record the changes.

Assigning Tasks

You can define a task that someone else is to perform, assign it to that person and get status reports and updates on its progress.

To assign an existing task:

1 Open the task and click the Assign Task button in the Manage Task group

2 In the To box, type the name or email address, or click the To button and select an entry from the Contacts list

3 Click Send to initiate the task-assignment request, then click OK to confirm the new ownership

4 The message will be sent, with a copy stored in the Sent Items folder

Accepting Task Requests

1 The task details on the originating system show that it is awaiting a response from the recipient of the task request

2 The task request appears in the recipient's Inbox

Hot tip

If the task is rejected, ownership is returned to the originator, who can then assign the task to another person.

183

3 The recipient opens the message, clicks the Accept button, then clicks OK to send the response

Don't forget

The task request is sent to the originator, and a copy is saved in the Sent Items folder.

Confirming the Assignment

1 The response appears in the originator's Inbox as a message from the recipient of the task request

2 When the message is opened, it shows the task with its change of ownership

The originator is no longer able to make changes to the task details, since ownership has been transferred to the recipient.

3 The task appears in the originator's Tasks folder, listed under the new owner's name

4 The new owner can change task details, and click Save & Close to save them, as the task progresses

Hot tip

When the recipient makes any changes to the task details, messages are sent to the originator.

5 When finished, the task can be marked as complete

6 For each change, the originator gets an update message

7 When the task is finally completed, the originator receives a status report with the task details (including total hours, if recorded)

185

Don't forget

Click the message box to list all related messages in the Inbox or Sent Items folders.

Notes

You may need a prompt, but the activity doesn't justify creating a task or an appointment. In such a case, you can use Outlook Notes. To create a note from anywhere in Outlook:

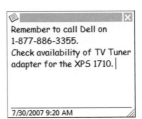

1   Click the arrow next to New on the toolbar and select Note (or press the shortcut Ctrl+Shift+N)

2   Type the text for your note in the form that's displayed, and it will be added to the Notes folder

3   Open the Notes folder from the navigation pane to see the current set of notes stored there

4   The note titles may be truncated so select a note to see its full title – the text up to the first Enter, or else the whole text if there's no Enter symbol

5   Click Small Icons to allow more space for the note title

Hot tip

Using category colors, you can associate different types of Outlook item that are concerned with the same subject or topic.

6   Right-click a note to select Categorize and assign a color category to the note

To change the default settings for new notes that you create:

1   Select Tools, Options, Preferences and click the Note Options button in the Contacts and Notes section

Don't forget

Settings offer three sizes of note, but you can click and drag an edge or corner to make a note any size you wish.

2   You can specify the note color (blue, green, pink, yellow or white), the size (small, medium or large) and the font attributes

These changes will apply to your future notes only – they will not be applied to the existing notes in the Notes folder.

Journal

Outlook can automatically record information about activities related to Outlook items in the Journal, a type of project log book.

Hot tip

If you want to track activities related to your contacts, it is better to use the Activities page associated with the particular contacts.

1 Select Journal from the navigation pane (or press Ctrl+8)

2 If Journal is currently not active you'll be reminded of other ways to track activities

3 Click Yes to turn the Journal on

4 Select Journal Options for items, contacts and Office file types to be recorded, then OK

Beware

If you do decide to use the Journal, limit it to the contacts and activities you really need to track, since excessive tracking can affect performance on your system.

Don't forget

Click the Entry List view to see the actual durations of the recorded activities.

5 The Journal begins to record the specified data, in a timeline format, as shown in the example below.

10 Manage Files

It is useful to understand how Office manages the files that constitute the documents, so that you can choose the appropriate formats when you share documents with other users.

Hot tip

Despite the visual contrasts between XP and Vista, most operations in Office will be the same. However, file management does exhibit important differences.

Windows XP Versus Vista

Although most features of Office 2007 are independent of the actual version of Windows you are using, there are differences to watch out for when managing files and folders.

To illustrate the variations between the systems:

 Open Word in Windows XP, click the Office button and then select Open

 Repeat the same actions for Word in Windows Vista

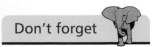

Don't forget

This shows the results with Windows Aero. The functionally is similar for Windows Vista Basic but without the transparency effects.

These screenshots show some minor differences. For example:

- The folder for Office document and data files is My Documents in XP, and Documents in Vista

- Access to the drives on your system is via My Computer in XP and Computer in Vista

- Networked drives are found in My Network Places for XP, and in Network for Vista

- XP, unlike Vista, has no direct access to operating-system file and folder search facilities

To see where the documents and computer folders are located:

1 In XP, select Start, All Programs, Accessories, Windows Explorer, then open My Computer, C:, Documents and Settings, the current username and then My Documents

2 In Vista, open Computer, User, current user, Documents

Finding Files

The search facilities are one of the strengths of Windows Vista, and Office 2007 takes full advantage of them. To illustrate this, suppose you've created a document discussing the Stayman bridge convention, but appear to have saved it in the wrong folder. To track it down, when using Office 2007 with Windows Vista:

1 Open Word and click the Office button and then Open

2 Click the Search box and type "Stayman"

3 Matching documents from the starting location, usually Documents (and its subfolders), are displayed immediately

4 Right-click a file and select "Open file location" to see where it is stored, or double-click to view it in Word

To locate the document when you are using Office 2007 with Windows XP, you must use the operating system Search facility:

 1 Click the Start button and select Search on the Start menu

2 Select "All files and folders", then specify the file type, a word from the contents and the location to start from

3 Click Search and XP will find all the documents that match the criteria

Beware

In the XP search you'll need a separate search to locate documents with the specified word in their titles.

Don't forget

Hold the mouse pointer over a document icon and the tooltip will show where the document is stored.

Recent Documents

Don't forget

Entries are displayed in the order of access, most recent first.

Beware

If a document is moved or renamed, the entry in Recent Documents is not updated, so it will give a "file not found" error.

Hot tip

To clear the list, set the count to zero. Reset the count to begin a new list of documents.

When you want to return to a file that you viewed recently, you may be able to select it from the list of recently-used documents.

1 Select the Office button and click an entry in Recent Documents to open that document

2 To change the number of entries displayed on the list, click the Options button for the particular application

3 Click Advanced, scroll down to the Display options, then set the number of recent documents desired and click OK

To change the file types listed when you open documents:

1 Select the Office button and click Open

Hot tip

Showing additional file types will make it easier to locate the correct document when you use a variety of file types in your applications.

2 Choose a specific file type or a group, for example in Word you can choose All Word Documents

Don't forget

You can have more than one document with the same name, if you have, for example, Office 2007 and Office 2003 versions.

Charles Dickens by George Orwell
Charles Dickens by George Orwell

Charles Dickens by George Orwell.doc
Charles Dickens by George Orwell.docx

3 You may need to change Folder Options (see page 22) to show the file extensions for the file types you've selected

XML File Formats

Office 2007 introduces new file formats that are based on XML. They apply to Word 2007, Excel 2007 and PowerPoint 2007. The XML file types include:

Application	XML file type	Extension
Word	Document	.docx
	Macro-enabled document	.docm
	Template	.dotx
	Macro-enabled template	.dotm
Excel	Workbook	.xlsx
	Macro-enabled workbook	.xlsm
	Template	.xltx
	Macro-enabled template	.xltm
	Non-XML binary workbook	.xlsb
	Macro-enabled add-in	.xlam
PowerPoint	Presentation	.pptx
	Macro-enabled presentation	.pptm
	Template	.potx
	Macro-enabled template	.potm
	Macro-enabled add-in	.ppam
	Show	.ppsx
	Macro-enabled show	.ppsm
	Slide	.sldx
	Macro-enabled slide	.sldm
	Office theme	.thmx

The benefits of using the new file formats are:

● Document Size

The new formats are automatically compressed and can be up to 75% smaller, saving disk space and reducing transmission sizes when you send files via email, over networks or across the Internet.

● Document Recovery

Files are structured in a modular fashion that keeps different data components in the file separate from each other. This allows files to be opened even if a component within the file (for example, a chart or table) is damaged or corrupted (see page 204).

● Macro Management

Files saved using the default "x" suffix (such as .docx, .xlsx, and .pptx) cannot contain executable Visual Basic for Applications (VBA) macros or XLM macros. Only files using the "m" suffix (e.g. .docm, .xlsm, and .pptm) can contain such macros.

● Privacy

Personally identifiable information and business-sensitive information, such as author names, comments, tracked changes, and file paths, can be identified and removed using Document Inspector (see page 214).

Compatibility

To maintain compatibility, Office 2007 can read, edit and save files in the original binary file formats used by older versions of Office. This allows you to create documents in formats that other users can work with, even if they don't have Office 2007.

Alternatively, those users can download the Compatibility Pack:

1 Go to www.microsoft.com/downloads and search for Microsoft Office Compatibility Pack for Office 2007

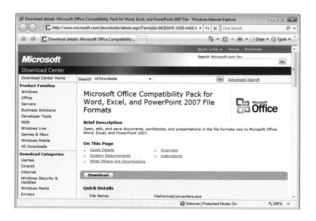

2 Click Download and follow the prompts to download and install the file-format converters

Don't forget

This means that you can avoid receiving files with hidden and unexpected macros that could otherwise potentially affect the integrity of your data.

Beware

For the converters to work, the users must update their versions of Microsoft Office to the appropriate service level:
Office 2000 SP3
Office XP SP3
Office 2003 SP1

Hot tip

With these converters, users of older versions of Office can create, edit and save documents in the new XML formats.

Save As PDF or XPS

There are times when you'd like to allow other users to view and print your documents, but you'd rather they didn't make changes. These could include résumés, legal documents, newsletters or any other documents that are meant for review only. Office 2007 provides for this situation, with add–ins for two file formats.

Portable Document Format (PDF)

PDF is a fixed-layout file format that preserves your document formatting when the file is viewed online or printed, while the data in the file cannot be easily changed. The PDF format is also useful for documents that will be published using commercial printing methods.

XML Paper Specification (XPS)

XPS also preserves document formatting and protects the data content. However, it is not yet widely used. The XPS format ensures that when the file is viewed online or printed, it retains exactly the format that you intended, and that data in the file cannot be easily changed.

Before you can save documents in either format, you must install the appropriate add-in.

PDF was developed and is supported by Adobe, which provides a free Reader for viewing and printing PDF files. XPS is a competitive product from Microsoft, who also provide a free XPS viewer.

1. Visit www.microsoft.com/downloads and search for "Microsoft Save as PDF or XPS"

This finds the add-in that supports both formats. If you'll only ever use one of them, you can search for "Microsoft Save as PDF" or "Microsoft Save as XPS", as appropriate.

2. Click Download and follow the prompts to begin the installation of the file-format add-in

3 Click the Run button and Windows will configure and install the add-in

4 With the document open, click the Office button, move to Save As and click PDF or XPS

199

5 Choose PDF or XPS (for dual add-ins), then Publish

Fonts in Office 2007

There are a number of new fonts provided with Windows Vista and Office 2007, including Calibri, Cambria, Candara, Consolas, Constantia, Corbel, Nyala and Segoe. You can preview text using these fonts or any of the Windows fonts:

1 Select the text to be previewed, then select the Home tab

200

2 Click the arrow in the Font box and move the mouse pointer over a Font name to see an immediate preview

3 Click the desired font name to put the change into effect

This helps indicate how the text will appear, but is an awkward way to explore the large number of fonts available.

With the help of a macro available from Microsoft, you can create
a document that provides a sample of every font on your system.

 Visit support.microsoft.com/kb/209205

Hot tip

There are two macros.
ListFonts creates a
document with samples
for each font. ListAllFonts
provides similar
content but in a
neater table format.

2 Scroll down to ListAllFonts and select the code

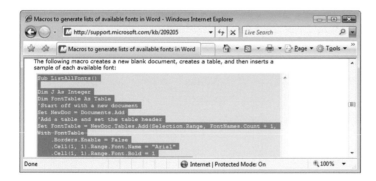

Don't forget

Highlight all the lines of
code, ready for copying,
from the first line
    Sub ListAllFonts()
to the last line
    End Sub

3 Open a new blank document and select the View tab

Create and Run ListAllMacros

Hot tip

Just clicking the Macros button will select and carry out the View Macros action.

1 Click the arrow on the Macros button in the Macros group and select the View Macros entry

2 Name the macro ListAllMacros, choose "Macros in" Document1 and click the Create button

3 Highlight the skeleton code

```
Sub ListAllFonts()

Dim J As Integer
Dim FontTable As Table
'Start off with a new document
Set NewDoc = Documents.Add
'Add a table and set the table header
Set FontTable = NewDoc.Tables.Add(Selection.Range, FontNames.Count + 1, 2)
With FontTable
    .Borders.Enable = False
    .Cell(1, 1).Range.Font.Name = "Arial"
    .Cell(1, 1).Range.Font.Bold = 1
    .Cell(1, 1).Range.InsertAfter "Font Name"
    .Cell(1, 2).Range.Font.Name = "Arial"
    .Cell(1, 2).Range.Font.Bold = 1
    .Cell(1, 2).Range.InsertAfter "Font Example"
End With
'Go through all the fonts and add them to the table
For J = 1 To FontNames.Count
    With FontTable
        .Cell(J + 1, 1).Range.Font.Name = "Arial"
        .Cell(J + 1, 1).Range.Font.Size = 10
        .Cell(J + 1, 1).Range.InsertAfter FontNames(J)
        .Cell(J + 1, 2).Range.Font.Name = FontNames(J)
        .Cell(J + 1, 2).Range.Font.Size = 10
        .Cell(J + 1, 2).Range.InsertAfter "ABCDEFG abcdefg 1234567890"
    End With
Next J
FontTable.Sort SortOrder:=wdSortOrderAscending
End Sub
```

Don't forget

This saves the macro into the current document, ready to run.

4 Copy and paste the code from the Microsoft website, then select File, Close and Return to Microsoft Word

File	
Save Normal	Ctrl+S
Import File...	Ctrl+M
Export File...	Ctrl+E
Remove	
Print...	Ctrl+P
Close and Return to Microsoft Word	Alt+Q

5 Select View Macros again, click the macro name and select Run

6 A new document is created and the font samples are inserted

7 Save the document to keep the list of font samples for future reference

Document Recovery

Sometimes your system may, for one reason or another, close down before you have saved the changes on the document you were working on. The next time you start the application concerned, the Document Recovery feature will recover as much as possible of the work you'd carried out since you last saved it.

1 Open the application (in this case Word) in the usual way

2 View the versions offered and choose the one nearest to your requirement, then save that version

By default, your document is automatically saved every ten minutes, but you can change how frequently this is carried out:

1 Click the Office button, select the Options button for that application, then click the Save entry, adjust the timing and click OK

11 Up to Date and Secure

Microsoft Update makes sure that you take advantage of updates to Office. You can also get the latest information and guidance with online help. Office also enables you to protect your documents appropriately and to secure your system.

Enable Updates

Don't forget

For other Office applications, including OneNote, Outlook and Publisher, select Help from the menu bar, then click Check for Updates.

For an application using the Ribbon technology (Access, Excel, PowerPoint, or Word):

1 Click the Microsoft Office button and click the Options button for the application, e.g. Word Options

2 Click Resources and then click Check for Updates

3 You will be invited to install Microsoft Update, which will automatically update both Windows and Office

Hot tip

If there's more than one user defined on your computer, all users will benefit from the updates, whichever user installs Microsoft Update.

4 Click Install to download and install Microsoft Update

5 When installation is complete, you can access Microsoft
Update via the Windows Update entry in the Start menu

There's a similar procedure for installing Microsoft Update for
Office 2007 running under Windows XP, but in this case a new
Microsoft Update entry is placed in the Start menu.

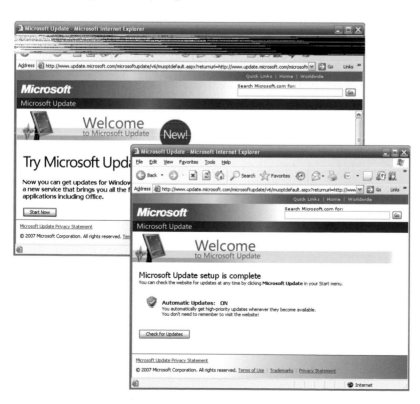

Don't forget

Microsoft Update will run
automatically at the set
time, but you can invoke
the update manually if
you want to get your
system up to date
immediately.

Run Microsoft Update

Hot tip

In Windows XP, you'd select the Start menu option Microsoft Update.

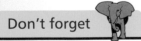

1 Click Start, All Programs, select Windows Update and click the link Check for Updates

2 If updates are found, click Install Updates to apply them to your system

3 You should select all the updates that are marked as important – ten updates for Office in this illustration

Don't forget

Microsoft Update will offer updates only for the specific Office applications that are installed on your system.

Name	Type	Published
CAPICOM (1)		
☑ Security Update for CAPICOM (KB931906)	Important	5/8/2007
Windows Vista (1)		
☐ Update for Windows Vista (KB929735)	Optional	1/29/2007
Office 2007 (10)		
☑ Security Update for Microsoft Office Excel 2007 (KB936509)	Important	7/10/2007
☑ Security Update for Microsoft Office Publisher 2007 (KB936646)	Important	7/10/2007

Choose the updates you want to install
Total available: 27 updates

Total selected: 11 updates

Install   Cancel

4   Microsoft Update will begin installing the updates

5   There's usually no interaction required, but you can stop the installation at any time if you wish

6   Select Office, Options, Resources and click the About button in a Ribbon-based application, or select Help, About for other applications, to see the release level

About Microsoft Office Outlook

Microsoft® Office Outlook® 2007 (12.0.4518.1014) MSO (12.0.4518.1014)
Part of Microsoft Office Ultimate 2007
© 2006 Microsoft Corporation. All rights reserved.

About Microsoft Office Outlook

Microsoft® Office Outlook® 2007 (12.0.6023.5000) MSO (12.0.6017.5000)
Part of Microsoft Office Ultimate 2007
© 2006 Microsoft Corporation. All rights reserved.

Beware

Sometimes an update may require you to accept the associated terms and conditions before it can proceed.

Don't forget

This shows the change in version and release levels for Outlook as shipped and after running Microsoft Update for the first time.

Office Help

There are several ways to display Office Help for an application.

1 Click on the tab row or 🔘 on the toolbar

Hot tip

Menu bar and toolbar Help options are provided in non-Ribbon applications such as OneNote, Outlook and Publisher.

2 Press F1 on the keyboard

3 Click Help on the menu bar and select the Microsoft Office Help entry for the particular application (in this case Publisher)

Help
Microsoft Office Publisher Help   F1
Publisher Tasks
Microsoft Office Online
Contact Us
Check for Updates
Office Diagnostics...
Activate Product...
Privacy Options...
About Microsoft Office Publisher

The Help window that opens is similar for all Office applications.

Back ⊙
Forward ⊙
Stop ⊗
Refresh ⊙
Home ⌂
Print topic 🖨
Font size A͞A
TOC ◆
Keep on top ⊙

Title bar   Toolbar   Search   Close

Type words to search for

Help topics

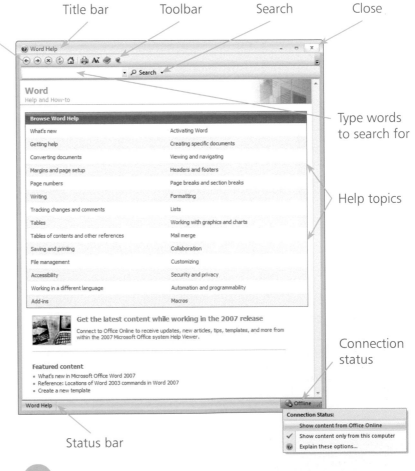

Connection status

Don't forget

To get the latest content for Help topics, switch to the Online option and link to the Office Online website (see page 212).

Status bar

4 Click the Connection Status button to change the selected option

Explore Help Topics

1 Click a Help topic to display its list of subtopics, then click one of the subtopics to display the contents

2 Alternatively, click the TOC button to scroll the topics

211

Hot tip

This shows that the topic "What's new" consists of three subtopics. The content is shown for the first of these, "What's new in Microsoft Office Word 2007".

Don't forget

The main topics in the TOC index expand when selected to show the subtopics. Select a subtopic, such as "Zoom in or out of a document", to display its content.

Online Help

1 Click the Connection Status button and select "Show content from Office Online"

2 If you have the table of contents displayed, you'll see that there are many new or expanded entries available

3 Click the arrow next to the search button to see the range of search areas available offline and online

Developer Reference

You'll see that the Search button in Help provides a link to the Developer Reference (in both offline and online versions). This information supports the Developer tab, used mainly by users who will be developing programs and functions for use with Office applications. For this reason it is normally hidden.

However, there are times when it might be useful to have access to features from the Developer tab, for example when you want to record a set of keystrokes as a macro.

To reveal the Developer tab (in Excel, PowerPoint, or Word):

 Select the Office button, click the Options button for the application and choose the Popular category

Hot tip

In Outlook, you'd select Tools, Options, Other, Advanced Options and then select "Show Developer tab in the Ribbon".

Click "Show Developer tab in the Ribbon", then click OK

Don't forget

Enabling the Developer tab for one of these applications enables it in all the other Office applications too.

The Record Macro command is in the Code group. The Developer tab also includes the command groups Controls, XML, Protect and Templates

Remove Personal Information

There can be more in an Office document than the information that appears when you review or print it. If the document has been subject to revision, there could be a record of all the changes, including original or deleted text and data. Any comments that reviewers may have added could still be there.

1 Select the Review tab and click Display for Review

2 You'll see that the file contains the original text, the markup and the final text

Office 2007 makes it easy to completely remove such information.

1 Open the document that you wish to publish

2 Click the Office button, select Save As and enter a new file name for the document

3 Click the Save button to create the working copy

4 Click the Office button, point to Prepare and then select Inspect Document

5 Allow headers, footers and watermarks if appropriate

6 Click Remove All to confirm for each item where data was found

7 When the items have been removed click Close and save the document

215

Protect Your Documents

When you send out a document, you might want to discourage or prevent others from making unauthorized changes. The Prepare function (see page 215) includes several options that will help.

1 Click the Office button, select Prepare and then click the Encrypt Document option

2 Provide a password for the document, click OK, then re-enter the password to confirm and click OK again

3 The contents haven't been altered, but when you close the document, you will still be prompted to save the changes

4 Now, anyone who opens the document will be required to enter the password and click OK

5 To remove an existing password, open the document, then select Encrypt Document as above, provide a blank password and click OK

If you simply want to tell users that the document has been completed and should no longer be changed:

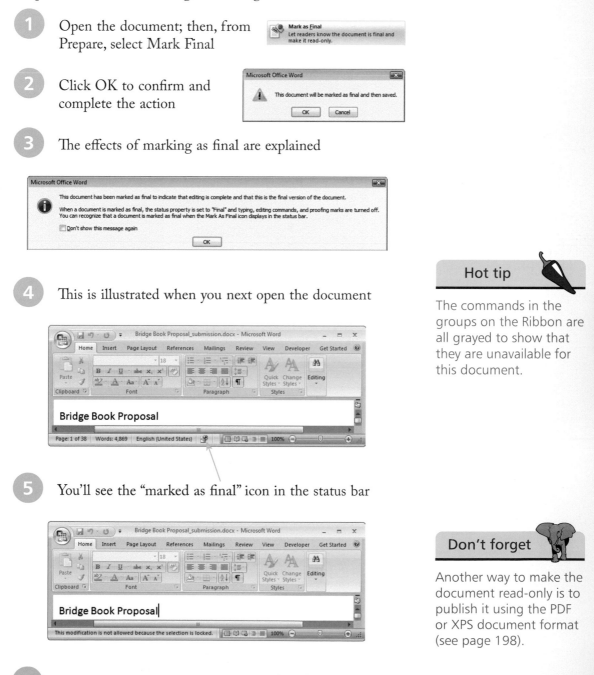

1 Open the document; then, from Prepare, select Mark Final

2 Click OK to confirm and complete the action

3 The effects of marking as final are explained

4 This is illustrated when you next open the document

5 You'll see the "marked as final" icon in the status bar

6 If you attempt to edit the text, you receive a message

Hot tip

The commands in the groups on the Ribbon are all grayed to show that they are unavailable for this document.

217

Don't forget

Another way to make the document read-only is to publish it using the PDF or XPS document format (see page 198).

Restrict Permission

If you have the Ultimate or the Enterprise edition of Office, you can go further and apply specific levels of protection.

1 From Prepare, select Restrict Permission and then choose Restricted Access

2 Sign up for the free trial IRM service

3 Follow the prompts to register for a .NET passport (or specify your existing passport) and sign in

218

4 The Windows Rights Management wizard will download an RM account certificate

You can choose a Standard or a Temporary certificate. It is usually more secure to choose the Temporary certificate, especially if there are multiple users on your computer.

5 Provide the email addresses for users who are allowed to read the document or to change the document

Don't forget

Anyone wishing to access the document will need to be online to access the IRM service to validate their credentials.

6 Those users must also register with .NET and Windows Rights Management or access is prohibited

Trust Center

The Trust Center contains security and privacy settings for Office applications. To open the Trust Center and display the settings:

1 Click the Office button and the application Options button and then select the Trust Center category

Tools		
Send/Receive	▶	
Instant Search	▶	
Account Settings...		
Trust Center...		
Customize...		
Options...		

2 Click the Trust Center Settings button and choose a category, for example Macro Settings, to see the details

3 Select Add-ins to apply more stringent control over these

12 Where Next?

Other Office Applications

We have looked at the main Office applications (Word, Excel, Outlook and PowerPoint) and the Office Tools in some detail, and taken a quick preview of Access and Publisher. Depending on which edition of Office you have installed, there are a number of other applications that you might have on your system. The full selection of editions and applications includes the following:

	Microsoft Office Basic 2007	Microsoft Office Home & Student 2007	Microsoft Office Standard 2007	Microsoft Office Small Business 2007	Microsoft Office Professional 2007	Microsoft Office Ultimate 2007 NEW!	Microsoft Office Professional Plus 2007	Microsoft Office Enterprise 2007 NEW!
Microsoft Office Word 2007	●	●	●	●	●	●	●	●
Microsoft Office Excel 2007	●	●	●	●	●	●	●	●
Microsoft Office PowerPoint 2007		●	●	●	●	●	●	●
Microsoft Office Outlook 2007	●	●				●	●	●
Microsoft Office Outlook 2007 with Business Contact Manager				●	●	●		
Microsoft Office Accounting Express 2007				●	●	●		
Microsoft Office Publisher 2007				●	●	●	●	●
Microsoft Office Access 2007					●	●	●	●
Microsoft Office InfoPath 2007						●	●	●
Microsoft Office Groove 2007						●		●
Microsoft Office OneNote 2007		●				●		●
Microsoft Office Communicator 2007							●	●
Integrated Enterprise Content Management						●	●	●
Integrated Electronic Forms						●	●	●
Advanced Information Rights Management and Policy Capabilities						●	●	●

For example, if you have the Ultimate edition, that could give you a total of ten application entries in the Start menu, plus the Office Tools and the Office Accounting 2008 Tools folders.

Accounting & Communicator

The extra applications are generally more business-oriented. The main functions and benefits are outlined, to help you decide if any of these products are necessary for you.

Accounting Express

Start - Microsoft Office Accounting

Microsoft® Office Accounting 2009

To get started, select one of the following options:

Start a Company
- Start a new company
- Import data from QuickBooks®
- Import data from Microsoft® Money

Open a Company
- Open an existing company
- Open a sample company

Restore and Delete
- Restore an Office Accounting company from a backup file
- Delete a company

Help   Exit

This is a simple accounting program designed to manage finances for the small or home-based business. The Startup wizard gives you step-by-step instructions, and you can import your existing financial data from other programs, such as Excel, Money or Intuit QuickBooks.

Communicator

This helps the members of your group or business to communicate easily with others in different locations or time zones using a range of different communication options, including instant messaging (IM), voice, and video.

The program integrates with other Office applications, including Word, Excel, PowerPoint, OneNote and Groove.

Office Communicator

Welcome to
Microsoft Office Communicator 2007 Public Beta

Sign-in address:
michael.price33@btinternet.com

Sign in as: Available
- Available
- Busy
- Do Not Disturb
- Be Right Back
- Away
- Appear Offline

Hot tip

The tools needed to sell online through eBay and get paid through PayPal are incorporated into Accounting Express.

Don't forget

Public IM Connectivity requires a per-user, per-month subscription license. This application is therefore mainly for use when real-time personal communications form a significant requirement for your business or organization.

Groove and InfoPath

Groove

This program is for working together on a project or report, with a group of people from different departments or organizations. You set up workspaces on your computer and share them with others in the team, and work offline or online, without having to worry about networks or servers.

InfoPath

With this program you can create electronic forms to gather data.

InfoPath forms can be sent as email messages, to be completed and returned online. The forms can also be filled in using your web browser. This could be Netscape, Mozilla, Safari and others, as well as Internet Explorer.

OneNote

OneNote

Being included in the Home and Student edition of Office, OneNote is clearly not just for business use. It is intended as a digital notebook that provides a single place in which to gather notes and information. Powerful search facilities help to locate details in the records, and the notebooks can be shared so that you can work with others.

Hot tip

You can search for information from text within pictures or from spoken words in audio and video recordings.

Don't forget

To help you get used to OneNote, there's a OneNote Guide notebook included, which has two sections: Getting Started with OneNote and More Cool Features.

OneNote deals with many forms of information, including text, pictures, digital handwriting, audio and video recordings. It supports two-way synchronization with Pocket PCs and Smartphones using Windows Mobile, so that you can exchange photos, voice recordings and messages.

Although you can run OneNote on any PC, it is especially useful when you use a pointing device, such as a drawing-pad stylus or a Tablet PC pen to add handwritten text or freehand drawings to your notes. You could even use your mouse.

Hot tip

Select Tools, Convert Handwriting to Text to interpret the notes that you have written.

This was (poorly)

written using

the mouse.

Other Desktop Applications

There are some additional desktop applications that are part of the Office 2007 system but are not included in any of the Office editions. These must be individually purchased, installed and activated. When installed, you'll find them added to the Microsoft Office folder on the Start menu.

Project

This is a specialized product that provides all the software tools and functions you require to manage and control a project. It handles schedules and finances, helps keep project teams on target, and integrates with other Office applications.

There are two versions – Professional and Standard. Project Professional includes all the capabilities of Project Standard and in addition provides collaborative-enterprise project-management capabilities (these are carried out in conjunction with the Office Project Server product).

SharePoint Designer

This is the web-page and website development product for Office System 2007. It replaces FrontPage, which provided that function for Office System 2003 and previous releases.

Its major strength is support for SharePoint Services, with their emphasis on collaborative working. However, you can still create general websites even if you do not have access to a SharePoint server. SharePoint facilities can then be added at a later date.

Visio

This is drawing and diagramming software to help you visualize and communicate complex information. It provides a wide range of templates, including business process flowcharts, network diagrams, workflow diagrams, database models and software diagrams, and makes use of predefined SmartShapes symbols.

Don't forget

Visio is available in two stand-alone editions: Professional, with advanced visualization features and data connectivity, and Standard, with a subset of the features and templates.

Samples provide Visio diagrams integrated with data to provide context. These will give you ideas for creating your own diagrams and help you decide which template you want to use.

Using MapPoint With Office

Don't forget

There are versions of MapPoint with a GPS locator included, so that the software can be used on a laptop for driving directions.

While not explicitly part of the Office System, the MapPoint applications can be used with Office applications. The latest editions are at the 2006 level, and there are two main products:

MapPoint 2006 North America
This includes detailed geographic coverage for the United States, Canada and Mexico (cities and major highways only). Other regions are limited to political boundaries and populated places.

Hot tip
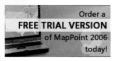

There's a 60-day free trial of these products available on CD or as a download. See www.microsoft.com/mappoint for details.

Order a
FREE TRIAL VERSION
of MapPoint 2006
today!

MapPoint 2006 Europe
This provides detailed street-level maps and address finding for the main European countries (e.g. France, Germany and the United Kingdom). Other regions (e.g. Bulgaria, Ireland and Poland) have some street-level coverage but no address finding.

Working with Office
When you install MapPoint, add-ins are installed into Office applications, so you can use MapPoint 2006 to insert maps into Office documents and presentations directly from the application. For example, you can use MapPoint to insert maps into Word documents.

1 Select the Insert tab, click the arrow on the Object button, then click Object

From the object type, select MapPoint Map and click OK

 The Word user interface changes to include MapPoint options from the MapPoint 2006 program

 Click away from the map, and the Ribbon is restored

Beware

You will need to confirm each time you open MapPoint, while you are using the 60-day trial.

Don't forget

Double-click the map to open MapPoint and redisplay the MapPoint menu bar and toolbars.

Office Server Products

For the larger business and organization, the Office applications can be used in association with a range of Microsoft Office servers. These are intended to facilitate collaboration, help automate business processes and improve management control.

The servers available include:

- Communications Server – provides a standards-based real-time communication platform that supports VoIP call management, audio, video and web-conferencing, instant messaging, and communication between software applications, services and devices.

- Forms Server – provides centralized management of InfoPath forms, allows access out using any browser, including mobile-phone browsers, and provides advanced controls such as "repeating section" and "repeating table".

- Groove Server – for centrally managing all instances of Office Groove in the organization, allowing the use of Active Directory for Groove user accounts, and the creation of Groove Domains with individual policy settings.

- PerformancePoint Server – allows users to monitor, analyze, and plan the business or organization, and includes features for scorecards, dashboards, reporting, analytics, budgeting and forecasting.

- Project Portfolio Server – relates project portfolios to make information available throughout the organization and aid data aggregation, visualization, analysis and reporting.

- Project Server – centrally manages and controls projects, with budget and resource tracking, and activity planning.

- SharePoint Server – supports central storage, sharing and collaborative editing of Office documents, which can be accessed by the associated Office application, by Outlook or via the web browser.

- SharePoint Server for Search – provides the ability to search file-shares, SharePoint sites and websites, and exchange public folders, Lotus Notes databases and customer repositories via protocol handlers.

Don't forget

The Office server products will require server hardware running Microsoft Windows Server 2003 (or a later version).

Beware

Some InfoPath controls cannot be used if the form has to be hosted on the Forms Server.

Hot tip

The SharePoint Server for Search can be upgraded to the full Sharepoint Server.

Trial an Office Product

The functions and capabilities can be quite complex, and you may find it difficult to decide whether a particular Office suite or application will prove suitable for your purposes. However, you can try them out before making your final decision. Most of the Microsoft Office products are available free for 60 days, so you can see for yourself what they can do.

Hot tip

If you find yourself at the wrong location, click the location button at the top of the page, then select your location from the drop-down box and click OK.

1 Visit Microsoft's website www.microsoft.com/office and you'll be switched to the Microsoft Office Online website for your location

2 Click the arrow to try the new Office free

3 Click the Try Now button for the product you want

Don't forget

As well as various editions of Office, you can download trial versions of Accounting, Groove, OneNote, Project or Visio.

Follow the instructions to register your details, then download and install the product. You'll be provided with a product key that allows you to activate the product for the trial period.

Test-Drive Office Online

The downloads can be large. Even the Home and Student edition will be almost 300 MB. However, you can try out the products without downloading them.

 Click the arrow to try the new Office free (see page 231) and then click the link to "Test it out in your browser"

(see page 231)

232

Click "Test Drive Microsoft Office"

Agree to load the Citrix browser plug-in if requested

Click the Register Now link and sign up for a Windows Live ID (or sign in using your existing ID)

5 Click the link to Launch Test Drive

6 The Citrix program opens a new Internet Explorer window and sets up the evaluation environment and the tutorials

Beware

The trial versions hosted in the test drive contain most of the functionality of the regular versions, but saving and printing of documents is not enabled.

233

Don't forget

You'll be given a reminder to download a 60-day trial, if you wish.

7 Select an application to try it out using the tutorial

Office Newsletters

1 At office.microsoft.com click the Help and How-to tab

234

Hot tip

Subscribe to the free Office newsletters from Microsoft to keep up to date with the latest information.

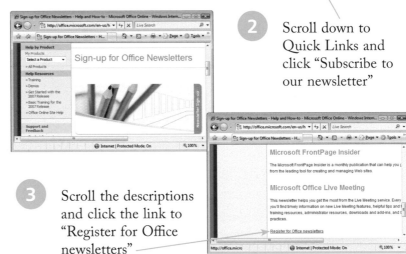

2 Scroll down to Quick Links and click "Subscribe to our newsletter"

3 Scroll the descriptions and click the link to "Register for Office newsletters"

Don't forget

Sign in using your Windows Live or Microsoft .NET passport ID to complete the registration process.

4 Select the newsletters that you'd like to receive

Index

P

Q

R

S

243

X

Y

Z